Jacob Piatt Dunn

The World's sSilver Question

Jacob Piatt Dunn

The World's sSilver Question

ISBN/EAN: 9783744730402

Printed in Europe, USA, Canada, Australia, Japan

Cover: Foto ©Suzi / pixelio.de

More available books at **www.hansebooks.com**

THE WORLD'S
SILVER QUESTION

JACOB PIATT DUNN

FRANK H. SMITH,
Printer and Binder, 22 N. Pennsylvania St., Indianapolis
1894.

The World's Silver Question.

I.

THE COINAGE CLOCK.

I take it that the adjustment of the coinage of a country is much like the regulation of a clock. A clock is regulated in order that it may run properly, and keep time, without any further tinkering than winding it up at intervals. A properly adjusted coinage will perform its functions without any tinkering other than the occasional addition to its volume to replace lost coins, or to meet the increasing demands of commerce. Ordinarily when a clock is out of order we send it to a clockmaker, but sometimes there is no clockmaker at hand, and such a concurrence of events brought about the great controversy over the village clock of Schnitzendorf, which is recorded in the Travels of Erasmus Wilberforce.[*]

This clock had been in use in the village for more than a century, and therefore was regarded with great affection and veneration by the villagers, but for some reason it began to lose time, and grew worse from day to day until it lost an hour in every twenty-four. A committee from the village council made an investigation, and reported that in their opinion the trouble was due to a wheel that had become worn. The village minister, who was about journeying to Nuremburg to attend the

NOTE.—Vol. 1, p. 196; Vol. 2, p. 83.

synod, was therefore authorized to purchase another wheel, but on his return announced that he could find no wheel like the one to be replaced. There were wheels of the same size, but they did not have the same number of cogs. There were wheels having as many cogs, but they were not of the same size. This report caused general consternation, and the village council was considering what to do next when Mr. Wilberforce first visited the place. I cannot reproduce in full the valuable debate on the subject, but will give a summary of its more important features, and persons of an inquiring turn of mind can consult his work if they desire details.

One gentleman was in favor of getting a wheel of the proper size, without regard to the cogs. He argued forcibly that the clock would not run properly if the wheel were either too large or too small. The village could not afford to be controlled by the fancies of Nuremburg clockmakers in regard to cogs, for if it did, Schnitzenburg would have to alter the clock every time the clockmakers introduced a new style of wheels. He believed in local self-government, and would never vote to submit to outside dictation.

Another member agreed fully in the spirit of the remarks of the first speaker, but insisted on purchasing a wheel with the proper number of cogs. He showed, by extracts from a work on clocks, that a clock cannot keep time unless the wheels have the right number of cogs, but that no two wheels were of the same size.

A third member regretted the tendency toward radicalism that had been displayed in the matter. This clock had been used by all the fathers of the village. His own grandfather had for years been entrusted to wind it. It had come down to them hallowed by a thousand sacred memories. It should not be marred by sacrilegious hands. As for him, he stood by the teachings of the fathers, and was opposed to any change whatever.

The speaker who followed also opposed any change, although he admitted that the clock was found to be half an hour slow every morning, after being set right the night before. He said that those who demanded the change were greedy capitalists who wanted laboring men to go to work half an hour earlier.

Another member, also devoted to the interests of labor, indignantly denied this assertion. He demonstrated that although workingmen went to work half an hour later, they were obliged to continue work half an hour longer than before on account of the clock's loss during the day. After a brief consultation with the preceding speaker, however, he announced that they would both vote to leave the clock as it was, provided it be set each day at 5 P. M.

The next speaker protested against any expenditure on account of the clock. In the entire history of the village there had been no such expenditure, and an over-taxed people would not submit to it now. It was agreed that the clock lost an hour each day, and all that was necessary was to direct the clerk to prepare a schedule showing just how slow it was at each hour of the day. The people could then easily calculate the correct time without any expense.

The economic policy was opposed by another member who maintained that an enlightened people never objected to necessary or beneficial expenditures. The people of his district believed that the clock needed a new key, and he had pledged himself to vote for one. He regretted to see that some members who had advocated a new key before the people were now opposed to it, but he proposed to be consistent, and to carry out his campaign pledges.

Finally Von Schermerhorn arose. He had the reputation of being a safe and conservative leader, and was supposed to be especially versed in time because he had long been the leader of the village choir. He said he was sorry to see such diversity of opinion on this important question, but must admit that there was great weight in all the arguments advanced. For himself, he was opposed to going to extremes. He had learned from the janitor, who had been making some experiments on the clock, that if one of the weights were removed the clock lost only half an hour each day, and this was conformable to reason because the committee had reported that the source of the trouble was the wearing of a wheel, and this wearing must have been caused by the pulling of the weights. He was willing to go to the extent of reducing the loss of time one half, and if the result was satisfactory to the people more weights could be taken off later on. He therefore moved that one of the weights be removed; that the clock be set at 5 P. M. each day; that the clerk prepare a schedule showing the hourly loss of time; and that the removed weight be placed in the village museum, with appropriate ceremonies, as a valuable relic of the forefathers. This judicious compromise met the general favor of the house, and was adopted without division.

Three years later Mr. Wilberforce was again in Schnitzendorf, and found that the controversy concern-

ing the clock was far more violent than before. Indeed,
it had become the one great subject of discussion. Instead of losing only half an hour a day, as predicted by
Von Schermerhorn and the janitor, the clock had come
to lose six hours. And this result might reasonably
have been anticipated if the council had carefully considered the proposal to remove the weight, for necessarily the reduction of the weight must make the clock
run slower. But error entrenched in law can be de-
feated only by long seige, and Von Schermerhorn and
his party stoutly insisted that the burden of proof was
on anyone who proposed a change to show that his proposal would remedy all difficulties, and as, in the absence
of a clockmaker, the question had to be discussed from
theoretical standpoints, a majority could never be
obtained for any one change. The party favoring a
wheel of the proper size had grown quite strong, and
yet many of them were ready to accept a wheel with
the proper number of cogs, without regard to size, as a
compromise measure. The essential thing to them was
to have a wheel. Another strong faction held that the
clock was of no real importance, as the clerk's schedule
was the real source of information as to time, and they
favored abandoning the clock altogether, and issuing
time schedules for the use of the people. There was
also a large party that favored taking off more weights
until the clock should lose twelve hours a day. This,
they easily showed, would make a day of twelve hours,
which would be a vast improvement because everybody
could do twice as much in an hour as formerly. It
would of course be a tax on employes who were under
a contract to work ten hours a day, but workingmen
had a tendency toward anarchism, and were unreason-

able in their opposition to an honest hour. This plan was advocated by all employers, who opposed with virtuous indignation the dishonest day of twenty-four hours, and so the system of removing weights had strong support, although it was producing an effect quite opposite to what had originally been claimed for it.

At length Von Schermerhorn brought forward a new plan for a compromise. He proposed that the clerk should be directed to inscribe on a piece of paper, "This is ten pounds, by order of the Council of Schnitzendorf," which declaration should be signed by the Mayor and countersigned by the clerk, and the paper should then be suspended in the place of the weight which had been removed. He said he had become satisfied that they had gone too far in removing the weight, but that it could not be restored because the janitor had unfortunately sold it for old iron. He was willing however to give the weight theory a fair trial, and thought that the council should yield to the general demand that something be done. After some discussion an amendment was adopted making the inscription read "twenty pounds" instead of ten, and the ordinance was passed, amid loud applause from the galleries.

During the few days that Mr. Wilberforce remained in the village the clock continued to lose time as before, but there was a general faith that it would do better when it became accustomed to the paper. The reader will doubtless agree with the learned traveler in regret that no information as to the final outcome of the clock question has been received. Those who are interested in such matters should procure his works and read his very thoughtful remarks on the difficulty of regulating clocks on a compromise basis.

II.

WHY THE COINAGE CLOCK WENT WRONG.

From time immemorial governments have fixed
their own forms of money, giving to coins such weight,
fineness, and relative value as they saw fit, and this was
necessary because every nation needed a fixed form of
money for its domestic uses, which are always greater
than the international uses, and no nation could expect
to have its coinage furnished by other nations. But
this necessity gave rise to disadvantages. Money is the
medium of international commerce as well as of domestic commerce, and when the merchant or the traveler
passed beyond the bounds of his own country he was
obliged to use forms of money differing in size, name,
quality and value from those of his home. In olden
times this was not so serious a trouble, because commerce was limited, but it grew as civilization grew, and
during the present century it has increased enormously,
for this has been peculiarly a century of development
of international commerce. The application of steam
power to transportation on both land and sea has given
opportunity for the exchange of surplus products that
did not exist before, and the telegraph has practically
annihilated distance, so far as communication is concerned. New York can communicate with New Zea-
land, or Japan, or India, or the Cape of Good Hope, or
Rio Janeiro, more quickly now than it could with
Washington in 1820. With fourteen cables crossing
the Atlantic, with cables circling Africa, Asia and South
America, and extending to Australia and the more

important islands, with wires ramifying every civilized country, and crossing some uncivilized ones, the world is in closer communication now than the towns of Rhode Island were at the beginning of the century.

As for international commerce, its spread, even in old and mercantile countries, is almost beyond belief. In 1800 the total annual international commerce of the world was estimated at $1,510,000,000. In 1889 the foreign commerce of the United States alone was $1,600,000,000, while the international commerce of the world was estimated at $16,885,000,000. The decade of the most rapid increase of international commerce was 1850 to 1860, when steam was being most rapidly applied to transportation, and the period from 1840 to the present is marked throughout by this development. In 1840 the world's international commerce had reached only $2,865,000,000, a gain of but ninety per cent. over 1800. In 1840 there were but 4,515 miles of railroad in the world—less than now in the State of Indiana—but in 1880 there were 228,440 miles. In 1840 the total horse power of the steamships of the world was 330,000; in 1880 it was 5,240,000. In 1840 the carrying power of all the shipping in the world was 10,482,000 tons; in 1882 it was 37,900,000 tons.* With this increase of commerce and cheapening of transportation, the annoyances and disadvantages of differing currencies were multiplied over and over.

The most important source of this trouble was the difference of standards of value, and this, too, although nearly all countries used the same materials, gold and silver, for their standards. The difference in size of coins, and the amount of alloy they contained, could

be overcome with comparative ease, because they could
be measured by the amount of pure gold or silver they
contained, but for various reasons different countries
fixed different relations between gold and silver, so that
the same quantity of one metal was worth more in one
country than in another. This should be clearly understood and firmly borne in mind, because it was the
greatest evil of the coinage systems of the world, and
the one that was most aggravated by the closer connection of the nations in commerce. One country
decreed that an ounce of gold should equal 15 ounces
of silver, another that it should equal 15½ ounces, and
another that it should equal 16 ounces, while in some of
the countries that we call uncivilized an ounce of gold
was valued at only 10 or 12 ounces of silver. Now in
each country the decree of that country was binding to
a certain extent, because in the payment of debts the
creditor was obliged to take any kind of lawful money
that was tendered to him, but beyond the borders of
the country its authority ceased, and gave place to
another authority. Therefore the merchant or the
banker would send gold to the country where the most
silver could be obtained for it, and send silver to the
country where the most gold could be obtained for it,
and so the coins of the various nations were drawn
about over the world as profit could be made from their
removal.

This fact has been observed for many years, and it
has caused an immense amount of trouble to various
countries at various times. The principle is commonly
called " Gresham's law," and it is usually stated in the
form, " Bad money drives out good money." This
expression is accurate enough in some cases, as, for

example clipped coin, if tolerated, will drive out un-
clipped coin, or paper money that is not maintained on
a specie basis will drive out specie. But it leads to
confusion if used in regard to the movement of coin
metals. For example, if England's coinage ratio of
gold to silver were 1 to 15, and the ratio of France
were 1 to 16, and both had free coinage of both metals,
the merchants and bankers would take an ounce of gold
from England and exchange it for 16 ounces of silver
in France, and, returning to England, would buy another
ounce of gold with 15 ounces of their silver, but it
would be absurd to say that silver was bad money in
England and good money in France, or that gold was
good money in England and bad money in France.
Nevertheless gold would be taken out of England, and
silver would be taken out of France. The more proper
statement would be that gold and silver move to the
country which gives them the greatest money value.
And this form of statement is the more desirable because
it makes easier an understanding of the expression
" market value " as applied to gold and silver, for from
this traffic in these metals it resulted that their commercial value was higher than the coinage value placed
on them by the countries least favorable to them, and
lower than the coinage value placed on them by the
countries most favorable to them, for the cost and
danger of transportation had always to be considered
as well as the matter of profit to the owner. Within
these limits the market value was affected to some
extent by speculation, by supply and demand, by new
discoveries, etc., but the chief influence was the force
of the combined legislation of the world, for legislation
fixed the ratios, and the coinage ratio of a country was
its bid for the precious metals for coinage purposes.

Some writers make the mistake of attributing all movements of gold or silver from one country to another to the action of Gresham's law. As a matter of fact most of such movements are due simply to the fact that these metals are money, or, in the bullion state, that they are designed for coinage. The chief cause of shipment is the settlement of balances of trade, and next to this is the advanced interest rate which one country gives above another. It is commonly known that when the Bank of England wishes to draw gold to that country the directors increase the discount rate, putting a premium on money. Other things being equal, gold is shipped in response to such a call, because, being less bulky, it is more easily and cheaply transported.* The simplest test of the question whether a certain movement of gold or silver is due to Gresham's law is a comparison of the money system of the country to which it moves with that of the country from which it moves, for of necessity no such movement can be due to an inherent quality of the money if the two countries have similar money systems. There can be no profit in traffic in money metals between two countries whose money systems are the same, but there may be at any time a movement of money for ordinary money uses. For example, the money systems of Great Britain, France, and the United States are now the same so far as the quality of the money is concerned. They are all on a gold basis, and all float silver and paper money on a parity with gold by maintaining gold redemption of both. They have different coinage ratios, but the market value of silver is so far below its coinage value in either of the three, that the difference of coinage

NOTE.—See Statement of Alfred de Rothschild in Proceedings of Brussels International Monetary Conference, p. 66.

ratios cannot possibly affect the market value of either metal. Hence it is certain that neither the flow of gold to England from the United States in the early summer of 1893, nor the return flow to this country a few weeks later, was due to Gresham's law. The outward flow was due to the payment of balances of trade and the premium on money in Europe. When our eastern banks suspended money payments, and issued clearing house certificates, money went to a higher premium here than in Europe, and gold returned, not because it was gold but because it was money. All money, gold, silver, and paper, was at a premium. Therefore, whatever might have been the effect of the Sherman law on our credit, it is beyond question that these movements of gold are not to be explained by Gresham's law.

But, to return to commerce, I have said that the effects of this difference of coinage ratios was enormously increased by the development of international commerce. Perhaps this may be more clearly seen by looking at historical facts. Lord Liverpool declared that, " The evils resulting from the fluctuations in the relative prices of these metals do not appear to have shown themselves in any great extent, or at least to have been the subject of general complaint, till the reign of James I."* This is probably true, though as early as 1553 Sir Thomas Gresham was complaining that the new commerce of England had increased the exchange value of " thirty-two shillings Flemish " from twenty shillings sterling to twenty-six shillings eight pence, and stoutly asserting that " plenty of merchants without experience is the uttermostly destruction of any realm."† The spread of English foreign commerce

* NOTE.—Coins of the Realm, p. 117.

†NOTE.—Froude's England, Vol. 5, p. 131, note.

under Elizabeth was great,* and by it the commerce in gold and silver as commodities, with countries having other coinage ratios, grew and produced its necessary effects on England's coin. The laws were repeatedly changed, but first one metal was exported and then the other, as the ratio made profitable. The effect on this traffic of the limited transportation facilities of the period may be seen from the following extract from the report of Sir Isaac Newton, director of the English mint, in 1717. After explaining that in England the bullion value of silver is greater than its coin value, the English ratio being 1 to 15.86—and that " When ships are lading for the East 'Indies, the demand for silver for exportation raises the price" by 1½ to 3½ pence per ounce, he says :

Gold is in Spain and Portugal of sixteen times more value than silver of equal weight and alloy, according to the standard of those kingdoms ; at which rate a guinea is worth 22s. 1d. ; but this high price keeps their gold at home in good plenty, and carries away the Spanish silver into all Europe, so that at home they make their payments in gold, and will not pay in silver without a premium ; *upon the coming in of a plate (silver) fleet the premium ceases, or is but small ;* but as their silver goes away, and becomes scarce, the premium increases, and is most commonly about six per cent., which being abated, a guinea becomes worth about 20s. 9d. in Spain and Portugal. * * * In China and Japan, one pound weight of fine gold is worth but nine or ten pounds of fine silver; and in East India it may be worth twelve ; and the low price of gold in proportion to silver carries away the silver from all Europe. So then, by the course of trade and exchange between nation and nation in all Europe, fine gold is to fine silver as 14 4-5 or 15 to 1 ; and a guinea at the same rate, is worth between 20s. 5d. and 20s. 8½d., except in extraordinary cases, *as when a plate fleet is just arrived in Spain, or ships are lading here for the East Indies,*

---

which cases I do not here consider. And it appears by
experience, as well as by reason, that silver flows from
those places where its value is lowest in proportion to
gold, as from Spain to all Europe, and from all Europe
to the East Indies, China, and Japan; and that gold is
most plentiful in those places in which its value is highest in proportion to silver, as in Spain and England.*

The fact that the coinage of a nation was thrown out
of equipoise by the arrival or departure of a few ships
was due to the slowness, irregularity and cost of transportation. The effects which Newton notes were seen
not only in England and Spain but also in the American
colonies and elsewhere.† As the volume of shipping
increased, the effect of commerce on the transportation
of metals grew so continuous and steady that it did not
cause sudden changes, and therefore did not attract the
same attention, but the effect was increasing—not decreasing. In this country the connection between the
movement of the money metals and the movement of
ships attracted comment even so late as 1833, when
Samuel Moore, Director of the Mint, reported to Congress, "The fact, indeed, is familiar at the mint, that
gold coins often remain in the vaults, unclaimed by the
depositors, until the day of the departure of one of the
packets for Liverpool."‡ Indeed the stability of our
coinage under the act of 1792 was largely due to
the cost of and lack of facilities for transportation,
for although we undervalued gold by establishing a
ratio of 1 to 15, there was no premium on gold in
this country that attracted notice until 1821,§ and yet in
the course of the next twelve years it became an intoler-
able nuisance, and Congress changed the ratio, by the

*Note.—Proceedings Paris International Monetary Conference, 1878, p. 317.
†Note.—See collected instances in Del Mar's History of Money.
‡Note.—House Doc. No. 38, 2d Sess. 22d Cong., p. 4.
§Note.—   "   "   "   "   "   pp. 2, 10.

act of 1834, to 1 to 15.98. This ratio was equally a mistake because it undervalued silver, and yet our conditions of commerce were such that it served the country very well for more than fifteen years. It is often stated that the new ratio at once drove silver out of the country. This is not correct. I know of no better witness on this subject than Hugh McCulloch, ex-Secretary of the Treasury, who was engaged in banking from 1835 to the beginning of the civil war. Speaking of his connection with the State Bank of Indiana, he says :

Although the double standard existed in the United States, the metallic currency of the country chiefly, and throughout the West exclusively, from the time the bank was organized, in 1834, to the discovery of gold in California in 1848, was silver. The capital of the bank was paid up in Spanish and Mexican dollars, and its reserve continued to be in this coin until it was sold for gold at a premium of about three per cent. on Mexican dollars, and six per cent. on Spanish. I had been a banker for fourteen years before I handled or saw a dollar in gold except the ten-thaler pieces which were brought into this country by German immigrants.*

Although this result quickly followed the gold discoveries in California, it was not due to them, but to a change in our commerce produced by railroad building, which fairly reached the eastern part of the upper Mississippi valley at this time. Before that our export was by way of the Mississippi and the great lakes, chiefly the former. Our import was chiefly across the mountains by wagon or canal, and then by the Ohio and wagon to destination. We sent goods down the Mississippi in flat-boats, abandoned the boats, and brought back silver. This silver was passed to the east for goods. It was the Spanish and Mexican coin in univer-

---

Note.—Men and Measures of Half a Century, p. 119

sal use in the Gulf country, and Spain and Spanish America had the coinage ratio of 1 to 16, as we did. Hence the silver did not begin to leave the country noticeably until the railroads put the east and west in direct commercial relations, with moderate cost for transportation to the seaboard. Then it went swiftly. In 1853 the drain had become so bad that Congress debased the fractional silver coins, and made them " token money," in order to keep any change in the country.

Another striking instance of the speedy action of Gresham's law in connection with modern commerce is seen in the case of Japan, whose experience is said by Jevons to present "the most extreme instance which has ever occurred." He says :

At the time of the treaty of 1858 between Great Britain, the United States, and Japan, which partially opened up the last country to European traders, a very curious system of currency existed in Japan. The most valuable Japanese coin was the kobang, consisting of a thin oval disc of gold about 2 inches long, and 1¼ inches wide, weighing 200 grains, and ornamented in a very primitive manner. It was passing current in the towns in Japan for four silver itzebns, but was worth in English money about 18s. 5d., whereas the silver itzebu was equal only to about 1s. 4d. Thus the Japanese were estimating their gold money at only about one-third of its value as estimated according to the relative values of the metals in other parts of the world. The earliest European traders enjoyed a rare opportunity for making profit. By buying up the kobangs at the native rating they trebled their money, until the natives perceiving what was being done, withdrew from circulation the remainder of the gold.

In 1860 the Japanese government, having observed the effect of commerce on its money, changed the coinage ratio to 1 to 13½, but this undervaluation of gold was sufficient to carry it away from Japan, as we shall see hereafter. To sum up the matter, the vast growth of international commerce had made it practically impossible to maintain bimetallism so long as various countries had diverse coinage ratios. The ancient system that had served very well through preceding centuries would not work under the new conditions. It had become necessary that there should be practical uniformity in the coinage systems of the commercial world.

III.

THE WORK OF THE COUNCIL.

The movement for the correction of the evils resulting from diverse money standards in different nations originated with the central countries of Europe, which suffered greatly from those evils on account of their close commercial relations. It is frequently stated that France maintained bimetallism at the ratio of 1 to 15½ for the first seventy years of this century without regard to the ratios of other countries. As a matter of fact France maintained that ratio, just as the United States maintained its ratios of 1 to 15 and 1 to 16, that is to say, its coins were drawn away or sent back according to the demands made by the ratios of other countries. That there may be no question on this point, I quote from the report of the French committee on coinage of the Universal Exposition at Paris in 1867, made by L. Mathieu and Baron de Hock. Speaking of the disadvantages of bimetallism under existing conditions, they say:

These are not idle or theoretical fears. The experience of France, and in all the countries having the double standard has demonstrated their reality. Before the discovery of the rich mines in California, in Australia, in the northwest of the United States, and in the British North American possessions, gold having a higher market price than the legal rate, the coins of that metal disappeared from circulation, and could only be obtained at a premium. After these discoveries, on the contrary, gold having depreciated below the legal rate, it was then the turn of silver to disappear. All the masses of silver, which the Bank of France had sought to accumulate at a great expense to obviate that result, were soon exhausted. The retail business suffered very much, and finally no other remedy was found but that of coining gold pieces of five francs (96 cents) and silver change of .835 fine.*

While these gentlemen state a fact of which they had personal knowledge, they do not state correctly the causes that produced this result. The real causes are mentioned in the report of this conference by Mr. Ruggles, our commissioner, though he appears not to have caught their significance, as follows:

The interesting fact is stated in a historical report (recently published by a member of the British Embassy) of the money of Japan, that it possesses a coinage of gold and silver in some essential features resembling that of France, particularly in a double standard, under which the ratio of silver to gold is fixed at 13½ to 1. It appears that, in ignorance of the actual relative values of the two metals in our Atlantic world, (of 15 or 16 to 1) these pagan Asiatics had fixed the ratio at only 4 to 1, which great exaggeration of silver they were furthermore induced to continue by a treaty in 1858, under which they were rapidly despoiled of their gold in large quantities by some of the traders from Christian nations. The partial correction of the mistake in 1860, by raising the ratio to 13½ to 1, (if any ratio fixed by governmental regulation be admissible at all,) shows an advance of intelligence in this distant region, inspiring the hope that, in due time, at least a portion of Eastern

NOTE.—Report of International Monetary Conference of 1867. Ex. Doc. 14, 2nd Sess., 40th Cong., p. 23.

Asia may be brought within a world-embracing and world-protecting belt of monetary unification. * * * The course of the monetary currents through middle and eastern Asia is instructively indicated by recent statistical returns from Russia, showing that of the gold and silver coin sent in 1865 from Russia overland into China, through the international *entrepot* of Kiachta, 3,876,184 roubles were in silver, and only 327,979 roubles in gold.

It was the high valuation of silver in the Orient, with rapidly increasing commerce,,that caused the silver movement of 1850-1860. During that period the average ratio of the metals at Shanghai was 1 to 14.34 as against an average ratio of 1 to 15.40 in the London market.* That means an average difference of 7 per cent. to cover profit and transportation. But when Japan was suddenly opened to the commerce of England and the United States, the market value of silver at once advanced, and during the year 1859 and the early part of 1860 maintained the highest average value that had been known for years. Japan's temporary coinage ratio of 1 to 13½ afforded an exchange profit of nearly 15 per cent. over the ratio of France. The brief-continuing ratio of 1 to 4 gave an exchange profit of 289 per cent. These advantages of commercial exchange explain the rise of silver, as measured in gold, in the European markets. That rise, in the decade mentioned, was only 5 cents an ounce, or less than 4 per cent. The great gold discoveries of that period did not depreciate gold as compared with silver. The general free coinage of both metals at fixed ratios prevented any such result. The real effect was a gradual depreciation in purchasing power of all money, as shown in the general rise of prices.

Note.—Report of Silver Commission, Vol. 1, p. 570.

The central countries of Europe, in pursuance of a
common understanding, first endeavored to meet the
growing evil by national action. Switzerland, Italy and
France debased their fractional silver coinage, but
Switzerland reduced it to .8 fine, while the other two
made their's .835 fine. In consequence the Swiss fractional coins were not received outside of Switzerland,
and on account of this inconvenience a formal union, in
which Belgium also was included, was formed in 1865.
The basis of this union was bimetallic free coinage at
the ratio of 1 to 15½, all standard coins being .9 fine,
with the five-franc piece (96½ cents) as the unit. No
gold coins smaller than the five-franc piece were to be
coined, and all smaller silver coins were only .835
fine. These debased fractional coins were legal tender
throughout the union to the amount of 50 francs, and
the nation issuing them was bound to accept them to
any amount. The coinage of the four countries was
made uniform in denomination, size, weight and form.
For coins above five francs, each nation was permitted
to issue gold coins of 10, 20, 50 and 100 francs, but
could not coin other values.

This system worked so satisfactorily that in 1867
an invitation was sent to all the nations to join in an
international monetary conference to be held in connection with the exposition at Paris in that year. Nineteen
nations sent representatives, and there seemed a fair
prospect of accomplishing something. They all agreed
that the diversity of coinage was injurious to commerce and governments. They all agreed that there
ought to be a system of international uniformity. But
when it came to the details of that system there was a
remarkable diversity of opinion as to matters that seem

to be of little importance. Most of the delegates were profoundly impressed with the advantages of the French metrical system of weights and measures, and thought it should be applied to coinage. There was an immense amount of talk about grams, and millimetres, and scientific standards, which was of little use, because measures of value are not only purely artificial, but they are also intrinsically different from any other measures in that they can never be permanently and definitely fixed. You might fix a relation between the weight or the diameter of a gold coin and the length of the earth's meridian quadrant, if the length of that quadrant could be exactly ascertained, but you could never fix any relation between the value of the coin and the length of that quadrant. Our commissioner, Mr. Ruggles, contended earnestly for a 25-franc coin ($4.82½), as that would be a reasonable approximation to both our five-dollar piece and the English pound sterling, which coins were as small as these two nations desired to issue in gold, but the Europeans objected to this departure from the decimal system in force in the Latin Union, and our Commissioner came home in a state of exasperation on that account. The most extraordinary thing about this conference, however, was the unanimity with which they decided against a bimetallic standard, which was the chief distinction of the Latin Union, whose success had led to this conference. Almost without discussion, they agreed to the proposition that international money " is attainable on the basis and condition of adopting the exclusive gold standard, leaving each state the liberty of keeping its silver standard temporarily." This proposition received the support of every nation but Holland. Silver standard

Russia, Austria and Prussia, gold standard England and Portugal, bimetallic standard France, Italy, Switzerland and United States, all voted for it. The only man in the conference who seemed to have considered the probable effect of destroying silver as a standard money, was Mr. Mees, the shrewd old president of the Bank of the Netherlands, who stubbornly insisted that, " He considered it inconvenient to adopt the gold standard everywhere, because it would reduce silver to change-money, and consequently gold would rise in value."

Very little came of this conference in the line of its original purpose. Spain, Finland, Hayti, Argentine Republic, and Venezuela have adopted the franc value (19.3 cents) as the unit of their coinage, and several countries, including nearly all of Central and South America, have issued coins in multiples of the franc value, but that is all. It was an error—an act of supreme folly—that the United States did not reduce the dollar to the five franc value (96.5 cents), and adopt a coinage ratio of 1 to 15½ in 1873, when we were using paper money, and when nothing but coin contracts would have been affected. But unfortunately our " financiers" were more interested in demonetizing silver than in forwarding the cause of international money. Indeed the same sentiment seemed to prevail everywhere, for the adoption of the gold standard became the common course, as will be seen from the following chronological statement of monetary legislation, and some events connected with, or affecting financial affairs:

1870. Franco-German war.

1871. Germany adopts law for gold standard, and stops coining silver.

1872. Denmark, Sweden and Norway decide for

gold standard. Germany retires silver coin. Payment of French war indemnity.

1873. United States adopts gold standard. Beginning of panic and trade depression that lasts until 1880. Germany begins silver sales. Panic in Germany.

1874. Holland stops coining silver. Latin Union restricts coinage of silver to $28,000,000 per annum.

1875. Holland demonetizes silver. Denmark, Sweden and Norway demonetize silver. United States adopts law for resumption of specie payments on January 1, 1879.

1876. Latin Union limits total silver coinage to $120,000,000. United States takes legal tender quality from trade dollar.

1877. Latin Union stops silver coinage and goes to gold basis. Russo-Turkish war.

1878. United States begins silver purchases. Japan abandons gold standard, and makes unit of value the silver dollar of 420 grains. Great trade depression in England. Failure of Glasgow City and West of England banks.

1879. United States resumes specie payments on gold basis. Germany stops silver sales.

1881. Argentine Republic attempts bimetallism at ratio of 1 to 15.3. French panic. Collapse of the Union Generale.

1884. Trade depression and labor crisis in France. Panic in United States.

1885. Egypt demonetizes silver. Panic in Argentine Republic—specie payments suspended.

1887. Turkey demonetizes silver, and prohibits its importation.

1888. Panama Canal collapse. Panic in France.

1890. Roumania demonetizes silver. United States begins purchase of 54,000,000 ounces of silver per annum. Panic in United States.

1891. Argentine collapse. Panic in England.

1893. Austria-Hungary resumes specie payments on gold basis. India attempts gold standard. Bankruptcy of Australia. Great panic in United States. Financial troubles in Italy, Greece and other European countries.

During these same years there occurred the most remarkable movement in gold prices that has ever been known, and which is shown in the accompanying table. The figures speak for themselves, but a word of explanation may be appropriate as to the "index numbers." These show the movement of average prices with reference to a fixed standard which is called 100. Dr. Soetbeer takes as a standard the average prices of 1847–50, and his figures show the average movement of price of 100 articles on the Hamburg market and 14 articles of British export. I use also the continuation of Dr. Soetbeer's figures from similar material as published by Prof. Taussig in "The Silver Situation in the United States." Mr. Augustus Sauerbeck takes as a standard the average prices from 1853 to 1877 inclusive, a period of twenty-five years, and his figures show the movement of price of forty-five articles in the London market. The London Economist figures show the movement of price of twenty-two leading articles in the London market. They were prepared by Mr. Newmarch, who takes for his standard the average prices of 1845–50 which were used by Jevons. These are usually given on a basis of 2,200, i. e., 100 for each article, but I give them as reduced to the basis of 100 for all, which is

TABLE 1.

U. S. Export Prices, Years ending June 30.

	Average London value of silver, per oz. U. S. mint.	Bullion value of a silver dollar at London price.	Index Numbers				Wheat, per bu.	Corn, per bu.	Cotton, per lb. Upland.	Lard, per lb.	Salt Pork, per lb.	Salt Beef, per lb.	Butter, per lb.	Eggs, per doz.	Steel Rails, per ton.	Cut Rails, per cwt.	Ohio Medium Wool, washed, per lb. Mauser & Avery.
			Average value 114 articles, Hamburg. Soetbeer.	Average value 45 articles, London. Sauerbeck.	Average value 22 articles, London. Economist.	Average wholesale prices, U. S. Senate finance committee.											
1872	$1.322	$1.02	135.62	109	129	127.2	$1.47	$.696	$.193	$.101	$.072	$.070	$.194	$.203	$112	$5.46	$.70
1873	1.298	1.00	138.25	111	134	122.0	1.31	.618	.188	.092	.078	.077	.211	.266	120	4.90	.55
1874	1.278	.98	136.20	102	132	119.4	1.43	.719	.154	.094	.082	.082	.250	.221	94	3.39	.54
1875	1.246	.96	129.85	96	126	113.0	1.12	.848	.150	.138	.101	.087	.237	.256	63	3.42	.52
1876	1.156	.89	128.83	95	123	104.8	1.24	.672	.129	.133	.106	.087	.239	.280	59	2.98	.41
1877	1.201	.93	127.70	94	123	104.4	1.17	.587	.118	.109	.090	.075	.206	.259	45	2.57	.43
1878	1.152	.89	120.60	87	116	99.9	1.34	.562	.111	.088	.068	.077	.190	.158	42	2.31	.40
1879	1.123	.87	117.10	83	100	96.6	1.07	.471	.099	.070	.057	.063	.142	.155	48	2.69	.38
1880	1.145	.88	121.89	88	115	106.9	1.25	.543	.115	.074	.061	.064	.171	.161	67	3.68	.53
1881	1.138	.88	121.07	85	108	106.7	1.11	.552	.114	.093	.077	.065	.198	.172	61	3.09	.46
1882	1.136	.88	122.14	84	111	108.5	1.19	.658	.114	.116	.090	.085	.193	.192	48	3.47	.45
1883	1.110	.86	122.24	82	106	106.0	1.13	.684	.108	.119	.079	.089	.186	.299	38	3.06	.42
1884	1.113	.86	114.25	76	101	99.4	1.07	.611	.105	.095	.072	.076	.182	.212	31	2.39	.36
1885	1.064	.82	108.72	72	92	93.0	.86	.540	.106	.069	.059	.075	.168	.215	28	2.33	.33
1886	.995	.77	103.99	69	93	91.9	.87	.498	.099	.069	.066	.040	.156	.183	31	2.27	.37
1887	.978	.75	102.20	68	101	92.6	.89	.479	.095	.071	.074	.054	.158	.163	37	2.30	.35
1888	.938	.72	101.93	70	99	94.2	.85	.550	.098	.077	.074	.063	.183	.159	30	2.03	.37
1889	.935	.72	106.13	72	102	94.2	.90	.474	.109	.086	.060	.055	.163	.129	29	2.00	.31
1890	1.046	.81	108.13	72	102	92.3	.83	.418	.101	.071	.063	.054	.144	.151	32	2.00	.38
1891	.988	.76		68	97	92.2	.93	.574	.100	.069	.060	.066	.146	.177	30	1.86	.37
1892	.871	.67			96		1.03	.559	.087	.072		.057	.160	.180	30	1.83	.34

obtained by dividing the aggregate averages by twenty-two. The figures of the Senate Finance Committee show the average movement of wholesale prices in the United States, and were prepared by the statistical experts in the government employ for the report of the committee to Congress.* It has been objected to the index numbers of Dr. Soetbeer and the London Economist, by Hans Forssell, ex-Minister of Finance of Sweden, and other monometallists, that they were unfair because they did not consider the commercial importance of the articles taken, and because a standard taken in the years 1845-50 was abnormally low. Mr. Nash therefore prepared tables, taking as a standard the average prices of 1865-69, and also rating each article in proportion to the total consumption.

TABLE 2.

Years.	Economist numbers, without reference to importance of articles.	Economist numbers, with reference to importance.	French numbers, with reference to importance.
1869-70	100	100	100
1870	91	90	91
1871	90	93	102
1872	97	100	105
1873	102	104	106
1874	100	108	97
1875	96	97	95
1876	93	99	95
1877	94	100	96
1878	87	95	91
1879	76	82	87
1880	87	89	88
1881	81	93	86
1882	83	87	84
1883	80	88	80
1884	75	80	
1885	70	76	

NOTE.—Report No. 1394, 2d Sess. 52d Cong.

The foregoing table shows the result, and also the result as to twenty-two articles in the French market, computed on the same basis.*

A comparison of these figures shows the same result as the original index numbers—a heavy and almost continuous decline of prices. The monometallist objectors might have anticipated this if they had stopped to think. The standard, in a question of relative movement, is immaterial, so long as it is fixed. If we should take the prices of 1773, or of 1492, as the standard, the relative movement would be the same. If we should take the prices of 1872 or 1873 as the standard, and call it 100, and reduce the others to the same basis, it would have no more effect than reducing a fraction to its lowest terms. The matter of use or consumption would be a factor of importance if we were considering the expense of living, but it is of very little importance considering the broader question of the appreciation of gold. However, that is immaterial for present purposes, for as we have seen the results are practically the same no matter how or when obtained. The student of social economy must accept them as facts, or deny all existing records of a statistical character. We may therefore proceed with the consideration of the money question, in the light of these facts, without any apprehension that they can be successfully questioned.

What did Mr. Mees mean by saying that the general adoption of the gold standard "would reduce silver to change-money, and consequently gold would rise in value?" The word here translated "change-money" is the French *billon*, which does not mean small coins,

Note.—A full explanation of this subject will be found by those who desire it in the report of Mr. Edward Atkinson on "Bimetallism in Europe." Sen. Doc. 34. 1st Sess. 50th Cong.

but debased coins or token money, such as is commonly made for small change. Such coin does not circulate on its intrinsic value but on credit. It is redeemable in something else by the nation that issues it, and that something is standard money, or money of ultimate payment. The use of silver as token money was no new thing to Mr. Mees' hearers. England and Portugal had reduced all their silver money to that condition. The Latin Union had made all coins below the five-franc piece token money. The United States, in 1853, had debased all its coins smaller than the dollar ; and every country represented in the congress had more or less money of the same kind. Of course, if gold were made the sole standard all silver would be reduced to token money. It would stand for so much gold. But why should that increase the value of gold ? The issues of *billon* had not affected it.

The reason is simple. More than nine-tenths of all the business of the world is done on credit—by checks, notes, bonds, open accounts, bills of exchange, etc.— and this credit creates a nearly constant body of debt. Some one is always getting out of debt, but others are always getting into debt, so that ordinarily the volume of debt is growing as the commerce of the world increases. Occasionally we have a period of liquidation, or hard times as it is commonly called, and then the volume of debt shrinks some, but commerce shrinks much more, and after such a period debt grows more rapidly. On what does this volume of debt rest ? The laws of every country give the creditor the right to demand payment in money. Lands, stocks, and property of all kinds are used as security for debt, but when the creditor enforces payment in the courts, this property

is sold and the money received is applied to the payment of the debt. No matter how much property the
debtor may have, he cannot compel his creditor to
accept anything but money in payment. In reality,
therefore, all debt ultimately rests on money—it can be
extinguished only by money if demanded—and in times
of general liquidation there arises a great demand for
money and a general shrinkage in the values of commodities measured in money. Economists have long
recognized this dependence of credit on money. Jevons
says, writing as to England alone:

While the elasticity of credit, then, may certainly
give prices a more free flight, the inflation of credit
must be checked by the well-defined boundary of available capital, which consists in the last resort of the
reserve of notes, equivalent to gold, in the banking
department of the Bank of England. Prices tempor-
arily may rise or fall independently of the quantity of
gold in the country; ultimately they must be governed
by this quantity. Credit gives a certain latitude without rendering prices ultimately independent of gold.*

But more than this, debt—or credit—does not rest
ultimately on all money, but only on standard money.
A large portion of the money of the world is credit
money. All paper money is evidence of debt. It is
the promise of some government, or some bank, to pay
in standard money. All token money is of the same
character, even though it may have an intrinsic value
that covers some part of its face value. Hence all governments and all institutions that issue such money are
in a constant state of liquidation, i. e., they must be
ready always to pay a standard dollar for the credit
dollar they have issued. If the pressure of liquidation
becomes too great, and they are unable to maintain

Note.—Investigations in Currency and Finance, p. 32.

such exchanges, they are said to "suspend specie payments," because the ordinary form of credit money is
paper. In such cases the credit money drops to a credit
value, or if it have an intrinsic value it may drop to
that value. When a country adopts the single gold
standard the only thing in which it can redeem is
gold, and it is under implied contract to redeem all its
credit money, whether paper or metal, in gold. In
other words it must maintain its credit money on a
parity with its standard money. In the United States
a question arose as to the intention of the government
in this regard because the act of 1890 provided that the
redemption of the "coin notes" by the Secretary of
the Treasury should be "in gold or silver coin, at his
discretion," and it was answered by both the great political parties of the country that they would maintain
all money on a parity with gold. The Republican
party demanded that "the purchasing and debt paying
power of the dollar, whether of silver, gold, or paper,
shall be at all times equal." The Democratic party
pledged itself to such "safeguards of legislation" as
would maintain "the equal power of every dollar at all
times in the markets, and in payment of debt."

At the time Mr. Mees spoke, the debt of the world
rested on values of gold and silver, constituting the
world's supply or stock, that were nearly equal, but
ultimate credit rested heavier on silver than on gold,
for there were only two gold standard countries in the
world, while there were several silver standard countries.
In bimetallic countries it rested on both metals, because,
although they issued silver token money, they also
issued standard silver money, which was money of
ultimate payment, not redeemable in anything else.

What Mr. Mees practically said was : If all the nations
adopt the gold standard, and reduce silver money to
token money, redeemable in gold, gold will appreciate
in value. Why? Because the volume of debt resting
on silver will be taken from it and placed on gold, and,
in addition to that, the amount of governmental debt
represented by silver coins will also rest on gold. Governments will be obliged to keep enough gold on hand
to maintain exchanges for their credit money, or they
cannot keep it at par. There will be a largely increased
demand for gold. The supply is limited. It must
appreciate in value. If you should kill half of the
horses in the world, the other half would appreciate in
value, because there is a certain amount of work to be
done by horses, and the decrease in number would make
an abnormal demand for those that remained. It is the
law of supply and demand. Increase the demand and
you cause an increase in value of the supply.

Was Mr. Mees right? Have the results that followed shown the correctness of his view? We find a
great many persons who contend that gold has not
appreciated, but that silver has depreciated. Let us
consider this. In the table on p. 27 all values are
measured in gold, and appear to have fallen. Of course
the appearance would be the same if the commodities
remained stationary and gold rose in value, because
they are measured in gold. On comparing the apparent
decline of silver with the apparent decline of other
articles, we find a remarkable uniformity between its
movement and the movement of average prices as
shown in the index numbers in columns 3, 4, 5 and 6 of
Table 1. Not only do they fall together but, practically,
at certain periods they rise together. Why is this?

Those who claim that silver has depreciated in value say that the depreciation is due to increased and cheapened production. If so, is it not a most extraordinary coincidence that its cheapening has been so uniform with the average cheapening of other things, and still more so that when other things grew dearer the cost of producing silver suddenly increased? Many advocates of silver make a somewhat similar claim. They say that silver has been " a steadier measure of value than gold." There is nothing in the nature of silver that would make it more stable than gold, and nothing in the natural conditions; on the contrary the demonetization of silver would naturally tend to depreciate it more than the average of commodities. This uniformity of movement is not a matter of chance. It is not due to any intrinsic quality of silver. It results directly and necessarily from the use of gold and silver as money. It is impossible that the value of silver should vary materially from the general average of values so long as it is standard money in a part of the commercial countries of the world, and gold is the standard money of international commerce.

Let me endeavor to make this clear, for it is a fundamental principle of the utmost importance. Countries that have silver as the standard money maintain free coinage of silver, and therefore silver bullion is worth what it would be worth in the coin of those countries, less transportation and mint charges, unless specially affected by speculation. In the daily market reports, for example, you will find Mexican dollars quoted at their bullion value, because it is practically the same to send Mexican dollars, or so much bullion, to Mexico. In silver standard countries silver is the measure of values.

When you pass beyond the boundaries of those countries both silver and other commodities are measured in gold. Suppose that at Vera Cruz wheat were worth a dollar a bushel in Mexican silver or sixty cents in gold. It would be immaterial to the merchant there whether he bought silver dollars or wheat with his gold, because he could exchange one for the other, and he would pay the same for one that he pays for the other. But merchants deal in other things than wheat, and wheat fluctuates in value from causes peculiar to itself; therefore the value of silver is measured by foreigners by its average purchasing power, and as in silver countries it is the measure of values its average purchasing power, and the average price of commodities are one and the same thing. Mr. Norman is one of the few economists who have perceived this truth, and with his characteristic devotion to " the exchanges " he maintains that " an altered relation of silver to gold necessitates an immediate adjustment of prices between countries possessing effective monetary systems, through the operation of the exchanges of gold for silver and silver for gold, affecting all articles interchanged between such countries." In other words the depreciation of silver would cause a depreciation of all prices. As he puts it elsewhere :

Is it not a fact that, upon a rise in the gold price of silver, prices of articles interchanged between a gold standard country and a silver standard country must be adjusted to the changed relation between gold and silver at once? Has it, or has it not, been clearly demonstrated that, in consequence of the higher silver price of gold in silver standard countries since 1873, the adjustment necessary has been effected by a fall in the gold prices of commodities, etc., imported from silver standard countries?*

NOTE.—The World's Metal Monetary Systems, pp. 98 and 164. See also pages 136, 152, 310.

The incorrectness of this explanation is shown by the fact that the fall of prices has not been confined to commodities imported from silver standard countries, but has occurred, on the average, with all commodities. A depreciation of silver could not affect prices in countries where silver is not standard money, any more than a depreciation of cowry shells in India could affect prices of commodities in the United States, or a depreciation of Zulu cattle could affect the price of dried fish in Iceland. Neither can an appreciation of the price of gold affect the prices of commodities in silver standard countries, i. e., as measured in silver under existing circumstances, and it has not done so. There has been a fall of prices everywhere if we measure them in gold, but there has been no fall of prices anywhere if we measure them in silver. The tables given show this as to gold standard countries. The testimony from silver standard countries is uniform. At the Brussels Conference of 1892, the stability of silver prices in Mexico and India was conceded by all. Mr. Denby, our Minister to China, has shown the same condition in that country.* The only complaint from those countries is the increased price of exchange, or in other words the depreciation of commodities and silver, as measured in gold. Gold prices dominate in international commerce, because gold standard countries dominate in international commerce. The commodities of silver standard countries are subjected to the gold measure as soon as they become the objects of export, and their price level, under the gold standard, is fixed by their barter or exchange relation to the commodities of the gold standard countries. Under the influence of universal

---

NOTE.—Consular Reports, No. 74, p. 508, No. 96, p. 317.

cheap transportation and quick communication, the movement of prices is practically the same throughout the world, the chief variations being due to speculation, which is at times made of considerable importance locally through temporary suspension of the ordinary effects of ready transportation. The "corners," and "stringencies," and "pinches" of the speculative world are local and temporary in character. As a rule the London merchant buys and sells by telegraph in America, Asia, Africa and Australia, and as a rule prices move under telegraphic influence. Not even the daily papers furnish information quickly enough for the business of this era, but in all commercial centres the "ticker" is an essential. Therefore we have a general uniformity of price movements throughout the world, and as silver's price in gold is controlled by its use as a measure of value in silver standard countries, we have in silver a steady measure of the movement of gold prices, except as occasionally affected by speculation. It may be objected to this that the movement of silver is not identical with the movement of the index numbers. It is not exactly so, because none of the index numbers cover all commodities. The important articles of real estate, live stock, labor, stocks and securities, and others, are not included in any of them, but it will be observed that the broader the basis of the index number the more closely it approximates the silver movement. For twenty years the price of silver has been merely the record of the total average movement of gold prices, and hence we may eliminate silver from the discussion entirely.

Suppose that in the United States wampum were the standard money. The price which the foreign trader would pay for wampum here would be the value of the goods it would buy, and the value of wampum abroad would be its purchase power here, less the cost of bringing it here. An appreciation or depreciation of gold would not affect its purchasing power. If goods go up abroad wampum goes up. If goods go down abroad, wampum goes down. But if for any reason there should be a change that affected wampum alone, it would be shown at once in prices here. If a cheap process of making it were discovered, wampum would go down and goods would go up. And so it is with silver. So long as that metal retains its old relation to the average of prices, it is evident that its appreciation or depreciation measured in gold merely registers either a change in gold or a change in the average of commodities. The real question is whether gold has appreciated or the average value of all commodities has depreciated. There are some economists who hold that "the appreciation of gold and the depreciation of prices are one and the same thing." They are the same in but one respect—they show the same result when gold is used as the measure. But it is important to know which movement has occurred, for if gold has appreciated it is evidently due to the governmental action of demonetizing silver, while if prices have depreciated it has been due to a cheapening of production or to some sort of natural increase of supply. If the latter be true there is no remedy, and should be none. If the former be true we should inquire if the result is detrimental, and if so governments should correct the evil.

Let us consider the evidence as to which movement has occurred. In the first place there appears an adequate cause for the appreciation of gold, but no adequate cause for a general depreciation of commodities. For 1890 the world's stock of the precious metals is estimated by Mulhall at $6,175,000,000 gold, and $6,065,-000,000 silver, coinage value. The officials of the U. S. Mint report the production of the precious metals at two billions each, gold and silver, from 1873 to 1891 inclusive.* In 1870 therefore the world's stock was about four billions of each, and the credit of the world, treating the entire stock as money, rested on eight billions of gold and silver. The silver money stock of silver standard countries is now estimated by our mint officials at $985,000,000.† All the remainder of the silver money of the world is token money, on a gold basis. The credit of the world therefore rests on a metal stock of six billions gold and one billion silver. Of course the coin, or money stock, is considerably less than the total metal stock, and there is certainly a larger percentage of the metal stock in coin now than there was in 1870, for coinage has been in excess of production during these twenty years, as is shown in Appendix 1, but it can hardly be doubted that the volume of standard money in the world is less now than it was in 1870. But while the amount of standard money has decreased, or at the least has not increased, the volume of debt has increased rapidly. The period from 1870 to 1890 has been one of great enterprise and great extension of commerce, improvement, and everything that would naturally make debt. International commerce has increased over 50 per cent. Domestic commerce has increased much more. Railroad mileage has increased about 200 per cent. The development of

*NOTE.—See Appendix 1, also "Coinage Laws," 3d Ed., p. 95.
†NOTE.—See Appendix 2.

new countries has been enormous. In addition to the
natural growth of debt from these causes, we now have
an additional burden of three billions of token money
silver, and an increased issue of about two billions of
paper money resting on the standard money stock, or
practically on gold. It is difficult to get any just con-
ception of the amount of the world's debt. The last
census gives the total national debts of the world at
twenty-seven billions in 1890, and seventeen billions in
1870. The same authority fixes the total public debt
of the United States at two billions, of which 892 millions is national. It is certain that in this country the
bank debt is greater than the total public debt; the
railroad debt is greater than the bank debt; the private
mortgage debt is greater than the railroad debt; and
the open debt is greater than the mortgage debt. Pre-
sumably similar conditions exist elsewhere, and we may
safely assume that the volume of the world's debt is
not less than 300 billions, and that the private debt has
increased from 1870 to 1890 no less rapidly than the
national debts.*

This relative shrinkage of the base on which debt
rests, and by which it must ultimately be extinguished,
furnishes a reasonable explanation for the increase in
value of that base, but, on the other hand, where is an
explanation for a general fall in the values of commod-

NOTE.—Statistical returns indicate this. The mortgage debt of the "small
holdings" of peasants of Austria-Hungary increased 41.89 per cent. from 1867 to 1888.
The farm mortgages of Denmark show an increase since 1870 equal to 7 per cent. of
the value of the estates. The increase of such debt in Prussia from 1886 to 1889 was
342,210,000 marks, or nearly 1.5 per cent of the value of the estates. The indebted-
ness of the peasant proprietors of the Netherlands increased from 959,948 florins in
1883 to 1,888,872 in 1887, or about 97 per cent. The mortgage debt of the agricultural
districts of Sweden increased from £36,507,064 in 1877 to £50,797,077 in 1876, or nearly
40 per cent. Publications of American Statistical Association, June, Sept., 1892, p.
181 et seq. In the Political Science Quarterly for December, 1893, Mr. George K.
Holmes makes a somewhat larger estimate of the existing debt of the United States
than is here presented.

ities in the past twenty years? There has been some cheapening of processes, but these apply almost wholly to manufactures, and such manufactures show a greater fall than the average, as, for example, steel rails and cut nails, in Table 1. But where is the cause for the cheapening of agricultural products? Is land cheaper? In some places, yes. But such cheapening is either due to an exhaustion of fertility, or it has followed the cheapening of products, which made its cultivation unprofitable. Productive land is not cheaper. Is labor cheaper? Monometallists say it is dearer, but we shall find cause to question that hereafter. If it is dearer it would not tend to make agricultural products cheaper, and certainly it has not cheapened sufficiently to cause any great reduction in prices. Have we had any revolution in agricultural machinery in twenty years? No; we had reapers, and mowers, and threshers in 1870. There has been an improvement of machinery in some respects, but nothing that could make any such reductions of prices as has occurred. Is the soil more fertile? No; farmers are obliged to use fertilizers more extensively every year. Is production increased? Yes; but not materially more than consumption. Is transportation cheaper? Yes; it has fallen about one-half in the past twenty years, but the tendency of cheaper transportation is to reduce the price at the point of delivery and increase it at the point of production. If it were not for this, people in a new country would not make donations to induce the building of railroads, and farmers would not expend money for roads. As we have seen, prices have fallen everywhere. The prices of agricultural products, in Table 1, are export prices.

But, in the second place, while there might be some

question as to the aggregate effect of these influences on prices, the possibility that they have caused a general depreciation of commodities vanishes when we compare the period of demonetized silver with other periods. If there was anything to cause a cheapening of commodities from 1872 to 1893 it was improved machinery, cheapened transportation and new processes. But these causes were certainly as effective from 1850 to 1872 as they were from 1872 to 1893, and yet the average prices of commodities advanced as steadily in the earlier period as they declined in the later period. Examine this little table of index numbers of price levels from Mulhalls Dictionary of Statistics (p. 491).

TABLE 3.

Years.	Jevons.	London Economist.	Hamburg.	Soetbeer.	Average.
1845–50 - - -	100 -	100 -	100 -	100 -	100
1851–55 - - -	107 -	...... -	112 -	114 -	111
1856–60 - - -	120 -	127 -	121 -	125 -	123
1861–65 - - -	123 -	...... -	124 -	127 -	125
1866–70 - - -	121 -	140 -	124 -	125 -	127
1871–75 - - -	...... -	127 -	133 -	136 -	132
1876–80 - -	...... -	115 -	123 -	127 -	122
1881–84 - - -	...... -	105 -	118 -	124 -	116

Here are four independent records of price levels. They differ from each other in exact amounts because they do not include the same articles, but they all show a steady rise in the price of commodities to the period of demonetization, and a steady decline afterwards. There is nothing in the relative effect of cheapening transportation, improving machinery or advance of processes, that is not as true of one period as of the other. There is but one great distinction between the two periods, and it stands out so plainly that none may refuse to see it. In the earlier period the metallic money basis on which credit ultimately rests was increasing with greater rapidity than ever before or since, on account of the great gold discoveries in California, Australia, the Rocky Mountain region and elsewhere. In the later period the metallic money basis, on which credit ultimately rests, was decreasing steadily, as one nation after another demonetized silver and threw its burden of credit on gold. This affirmative evidence is as strong as could possibly be given in such a case, and must be conclusive unless some opposing evidence is strong enough to overthrow it.

Against it several arguments have been urged. The first is that the rate of interest has not increased. This looks plausible. If money is worth more, it would naturally command larger hire. The fallacy of the argument lies in the fact that the money paid for interest has increased in value as much as any other money, and therefore interest has increased without any advance of rate. Suppose that twenty years ago A made a loan of $100 bearing five per cent. interest, and B made a loan of 100 bushels of wheat at five per cent. interest, payable in wheat. This year both came due. A gets $200; B gets 200 bushels of wheat. A's $100 of interest has just as much appreciated value as his $100 of principal. B's 100 bushels of interest has just as much depreciated value as his 100 bushels of principal. The appreciation or depreciation of intrinsic value cannot be measured by interest payable in kind.

A second argument is that there is more silver money now than in 1873, and therefore no effect on prices could have accrued from silver legislation. Unquestionably the stock of silver money is largely increased. As shown in Appendix 1, the world's coinage of silver for twenty years has been in excess of the world's production. Of course a large amount of this has been recoinage, but there can be little doubt that there is now fifty per cent. more silver coin in use than in 1873. The fallacy of the argument lies in the fact that this silver is not standard money—not money of ultimate payment. The special report of the mint on August 16, 1883, shows a total money stock in circulation in this country of $1,631,000,000, or $24.34 per capita, which is more than we ever had before; but how much of it is standard money? The stock consists of $604,000,000 gold, $615,000,000 silver, and $412,000,-000 uncovered paper. Of this, only the gold, which amounts to $9.01 per capita, is standard money. The remaining $15.33 per capita is credit money, which the government is under obligations to redeem, i. e., to keep on a parity with gold. It was this fact, coupled with the facts that the government's gold reserve had fallen to the $100,000,000 limit, and that the government was issuing paper money in payment for silver bullion to the amount of about $35,000,000 per annum, or at the rate of thirty-five cents to each dollar of gold reserve, that precipitated the panic of 1893.

A third argument is that some prices have not fallen, and that if there had been an appreciation of gold it would have caused a decline in all prices alike. So far as it goes, the theory of this proposition is correct. The fallacy lies in the suppressed assumption that there could be no special cause affecting the value of any commodity that could counteract the effect of an appreciation of gold. This is manifestly untrue. Everyone knows that the price of any one commodity is liable to rise or fall under any money system. Although there was a general advance of prices from 1850 to 1870, and although it is conceded to be due to a depreciation of standard money, there were a number of articles that decreased in price in that period—as for instance, alkali, brass, candles, cement, coal, copper, glass, lead, paper, sugar, etc. The obvious explanation of this is that there were causes operating to cheapen these articles which more than counteracted the effects of the depreciation of gold. So, in the later period there are articles, such as coffee, India-rubber, and tin, that have advanced in price, although the average of prices has fallen. The explanation must be sought in causes particularly affecting such articles. The only movement of prices on which an appreciation or depreciation of money can be predicted is a movement of average prices.

A fourth argument, and one much used in this country, is that wages have increased, and that wages are the best measure of the appreciation or depreciation of money. This is akin to the preceding argument. It is founded on this teaching of Adam Smith :

Labour, it must always be remembered, and not any particular commodity, or set of commodities, is the real measure of the value, both of silver (which was then the standard of English money) and of all other commodities.

This theory of Dr. Smith has long since been exploded. David Buchanan, in his edition of "The Wealth of Nations," answers it thus :

The invariable value of labour seems a metaphysical notion, with which Dr. Smith has bewildered both himself and his readers. The value of labour is its market price, which varies, like that of other commodities, with the state of the supply. But if it thus varies

in its own value, how can it measure the value of other
commodities? Dr. Smith himself states that labour is
sometimes purchased with a greater, and sometimes
with a smaller quantity of goods; but he immediately
adds that it is the goods which vary in their value, and
not the labour. But why may not labour vary in its
value as well as the goods? Will not the price of
labour vary with its plenty or scarcity? And if it varies
in its own value, how can it be an universal measure of
value at different times and places? There is, in truth,
no perfect measure of value.*

The fallacy of Dr. Smith's proposition is almost
self-evident, for if you admit it to be true it necessarily
results than any apparent movement of average wages
is in fact a movement of money, and there can never be
any advance or decline of wages from any other cause.
The merest amateur in economy knows that this is not
true. In this country, one political party contends that
wages are advanced by a protective tariff, and another
that they are advanced by improved machinery, extended commerce, and steadier work. Workingmen
hold that the chief influence on wages is labor organi-
zation. No one holds to Dr. Smith's theory as ordinarily expounded. Indeed he did not always hold to it
himself, for he says :

The money price of labour in Great Britain has
indeed risen during the course of the present century.
This, however, seems to be the effect, not so much of
any diminution in the value of silver in the European
market, as of an increase in the demand for labour in
Great Britain, arising from the great and almost universal prosperity of the country.†

What Dr. Smith evidently believed was that, other
things being equal, labor was a good test of prices, and
so it is, but it was much more so in his time than now,
because the causes which most actively affect wages

now did not prevail then. But what has been the movement of wages in recent years? The best authority is the report of the Senate Finance Committee, which, taking wages in 1860 as a standard, shows the movement of the wage-level to have been as in the accompanying table:

TABLE 4.

Year.	Index Number of Wages.	Year.	Index Number of Wages.
1852	90.8	1872	152.2
1853	91.8	1873	148.3
1854	95.8	1874	145.0
1855	98.0	1875	140.8
1856	99.2	1876	135.2
1857	99.9	1877	136.4
1858	98.5	1878	140.5
1859	99.1	1879	139.9
1860	100.0	1880	141.5
1861	100.8	1881	146.5
1862	100.4	1882	149.9
1863	76.2	1883	152.7
1864	80.8	1884	152.7
1865	66.2	1885	152.7
1866	108.8	1886	150.9
1867	117.1	1887	153.7
1868	114.9	1888	155.4
1869	119.5	1889	156.7
1870	133.7	1890	158.9
1871	147.8	1891	160.7

These figures show a steady increase of wages during the first period, reaching at the close an advance of sixty-eight per cent. During the second period we have first a break in wages, and a failure to regain the original level for ten years; then a stationary period of five years; then a slow advance, reaching at the close an increase of less than six per cent.

over the beginning. It is certain that this slight advance has been changed to a decrease by wage reductions in 1892 and 1893, but that is not very material.
The essential point is, what stopped the increase of
wages that was in progress from 1850 to 1870? All the
known causes for increasing wages were even more
active in the second period than in the first. There is
no imaginable cause, aside from the appreciation of
money, why the advance in the second period should
not have been as great as in the first. And in fact
wages did increase in about the same proportion when
measured by their purchasing power, *i. e.*, by the average price of commodities. The retarded movement
appears only when measured in gold. The fact is, that
actual wages—wages measured by exchange value—
have advanced very uniformly from 1850 to 1891, and
that the check in money value is due to the appreciation of gold. These figures, however, cover organized
labor and skilled labor, which get the chief advantage
from improved machinery and new processes. When
we look at unskilled and unorganized labor, the result
is quite different. In this country the class of labor
least affected by these known influences, and most like
the labor with which Dr. Smith was familiar, is agricultural labor. Our government has made nine special
investigations of agricultural labor, at intervals, from
1866 to 1892, and the result as shown by the report of
the statistician of the Department of Agriculture is as
follows :

TABLE 5.

Year.	Monthly Wages Without Board.	Monthly Wages With Board.	Harvest Wages per Day Without Board.	Harvest Wages per Day With Board.	Ordidary Day Wages Without Board.	Ordinary Day Wages With Board.
1866	$26.87	$17.45	$2.20	$1.74	$1.49	$1.08
1869	25.92	16.55	2.20	1.74	1.41	1.02
1875	19.49	12.72	1.70	1.35	1.08	.78
1879	16.05	10.43	1.30	1.00	.81	.59
1882	18.58	12.41	1.48	1.15	.93	.67
1885	18.06	12.34	1.40	1.10	.91	.67
1888	18.24	12.36	1.31	1.02	.92	.67
1890	18.34	12.45	1.30	1.02	.92	.68
1892	18.60	12.54	1.30	1.02	.92	.67

It is evident from these recorded facts that if we make wages the test there has been an appreciation of gold ; but let us not be led into the belief that wages furnish the final and accurate test of the appreciation or depreciation of money, although the result favors our position. They are subject to other influences, and vary independent of the movements of money. Like every other commodity, labor has influences peculiar to itself, that affect it only, though the results will ultimately react on commodities produced by labor. The close harmony of movement between the gold price of silver and the gold price of any one commodity is a mere coincidence, not a necessary result, for the gold value of silver measures average prices, under existing conditions, and the harmony of price of any commodity with average prices, proves merely that it has not been subjected to any special disturbing cause.

In this consideration of the movement of prices, thus far, we have eliminated silver from the question. This was done for convenience, not from necessity.

That there has, in fact, been no decline in the value of silver from natural causes is evident from three facts:

1. Those who contend that silver has decreased in value assert that its production is enormously increased —the world has been "flooded with silver." In fact the production of silver, relative to the production of gold, has decreased. During the first half of the present century the world's stocks of gold and silver stood very steadily in the ratio of 1 to 32, *i. e.*, for every ton of gold in the possession of mankind there were 32 tons of silver. In 1849–50 began a great increase of gold production, and the amount of gold produced annually continued to be greater than the amount of silver until 1885, when the world's stock stood in the ratio of 1 to 18.4. Since then the production of silver has been slightly in excess, and the world's stock now stands at a ratio of about 1 to 18.8. This is the relation in weight. In market value the relation of the two metals varied but slightly until 1872, when the great apparent decline of silver began*, and in 1872 the weight ratio was about 1 to 20. It is impossible to account for a fall of silver, as measured in gold, by increased production of silver, when gold production was increasing more rapidly than silver production at the time the apparent decline of silver began, and continued greater than the production of silver for twelve years after. It would require a production of silver enormously in excess of anything existing, or in prospect, to bring the world's stock of silver back to the ratio to gold that it held in 1850.

2. It is contended that silver has decreased in value because its production has been cheapened. This

is not correct as compared with the production of gold.
The cost of gold mining has always been less than the
cost of silver mining, and it has decreased more on account of improved methods. It is well known that in
California and other places miners are now working
profitably the "tailings" or refuse matter of the miners
of 1850 to 1860. The improvement of method in
placer mining has been so great that gold dirt has been
actually treated at a profit that paid less than three cents
per cubic yard.* The difference in the cost of producing the two metals is chiefly due to the fact that gold is
usually found chemically pure, while silver is usually
found in chemical combination and mixed with other
metals. When pure, either metal can be separated and
collected by amalgamation with quicksilver, or, as it is
commonly called, the "free-milling" process. This, with
the possible exception of the collection of gold nuggets
by mechanical separation, is by far the cheapest process of separation known, and it has been brought to a
state of great perfection by improvement in crushers,
stamps, amalgamation plates, and other machinery.
There have been many improvements in the processes
of silver extraction, but all processes, except free-
milling of native silver, require repeated handling of
the ore, which is the greatest expense connected with
any process. Anyone who endeavors to get at the ap-
proximate cost of silver production will find a remarkable conflict in different authorities. The chief cause of
this is the inclusion or exclusion of the value of the
other metals found in conjunction with silver in these
estimates. More than half of the so-called silver mines
of this country could not be worked at all but for the

NOTE.—U. S. Census Report, 1880, Vol. 13, p. 201.

value of the lead, copper or gold they yield in addition
to the silver. Even the great "Bonanza" mines of the
Comstock lode are of this class. Their total product
from their discovery to January 1, 1893, was $141,986,-
344 gold, and $198,877,547 silver, but the dividends in
the same period, in excess of assessments, were only
$52,478,235. In other words, the expenses have been
nearly $90,000,000 in excess of all the silver produced.

3. It is claimed by many persons who are advocates of the use of silver that silver has depreciated in
value because it has not been coined as freely as formerly since 1872. This is an error. As shown by Appendix 1, the world's coinage of silver since then has
been in excess of its total production. There has been
no decrease in the demand for silver, but there has
been an increase in the demand for gold, owing to the
fact that it has been made the sole money of ultimate
payment in so many countries.

With these preliminary facts in mind, let us now
consider the advantages or disadvantages of the appreciation of gold.

IV.

THE CASE AGAINST MONOMETALLISM.

The reader will bear in mind that we are to consider this as a world question, with only secondary application to any particular nation. In the presence of
such fluctuations in the market relations of gold and
silver as have prevailed in the last twenty years, it is

impossible that any one nation should maintain bimetallism at any ratio. Each one must make its choice between gold monometallism and silver monometallism, if action is to be taken by each singly. Silver monometallism will never be accepted by the leading nations, and indeed it would be no better than gold monometallism if it were generally accepted. The world question, therefore, is between gold monometallism and a restoration of universal, or general bimetallism, freed from the known and avoidable evils of the old bimetallism. The position of those who are really entitled to the name of bimetallists, in my opinion, is correctly stated by M. Boissevain :

When, in the years immediately preceding 1870, M. Wolowski and M. Cernuschi began their campaign in favor of bimetallism, one after the other declared that the system of the double standard, to produce its full effect, must be adopted internationally. And since then the supporters of the movement have asked nothing else. Never, indeed, have the bimetallists desired that France alone, or the Latin Union, should go back on the decisions taken from 1873 to 1878. Bimetallism has always been defended as a system which absolutely requires to be adopted by a convention or an understanding of an international character. It is not too much to say that it is precisely this which distinguishes bimetallism from the double standard system of former times; in this respect it is even directly opposed to the old double standard system.*

In addition to fixing definitely what we mean by bimetallism, let us also summarize and bear in mind the following conclusions at which we have already arrived :

1. That the real evil of the old double standard system was the diversity of coinage ratios, and in a smaller way the diversity of size and alloy in coins.

Note.—The Monetary Question, English Ed., p. 49.

2. That this was the direct result of legislation, and can be cured by general harmony of legislation.

3. That during the era of demonetization of silver, or general adoption of the gold standard, there has been an almost continuous appreciation of gold, and consequent decline of prices measured in gold.

4. That this appreciation of gold is due to the increased burden of credit placed upon it by legislation, and not to any natural cause.

5. That the market value of silver merely marks the average gold price of commodities, and this is due to the legislation which makes it the standard of value in certain countries, and not to any natural cause.

The English monometallists concede the appreciation of gold, and consequent depreciation of prices. Giffen, the greatest of them, admits it. Norman contends as zealously against the theories of David A. Wells and his followers as he does against bimetallism. The records of the London Economist, Soetbeer, Kral, Sauerbeck, and others, are sufficient for them. In no preceding period were statistics gathered so carefully. In none was there such striking agreement in the results wherever and by whomsoever ascertained. The figures speak for themselves. If we cannot believe them we cannot rely on statistics for anything. The chief argument of the English monometallists is that a restoration of bimetallism would be an injury to the creditor class. In the sense that creditors would receive payment for existing debt in money that would have less purchasing power than the same quantity now has is true, because the purchasing power of money has been artificially increased by the demonetization of silver. But if any real injury resulted from this, which is

improbable, it would necessarily be offset by the benefit
received by the debtor class. Who constitute the creditor
class and who the debtor class? The number holding
fixed and exclusive relations with either is so small as
to be insignificant. Every man who transacts business
is to some extent a debtor, and to some extent a creditor,
and it is from this fact that the great evil of the legislation towards a general gold standard has resulted. For
twenty years the world has been transacting business
on a falling market. There have been some reactions,
and there have been some lines of business that have
not been thus affected, but on the average there has
been a remarkably steady trend downwards—indeed the
most remarkable movement of that kind the world has
ever known. There are few business men who do not
understand the injurious effects of a falling market in
their own affairs. The merchant buys goods on credit;
the wholesale price goes down ; he is forced to compete
with merchants who have bought later at lower prices ;
legitimate profits are reduced ; debt and interest are not
reduced. The manufacturer estimates the cost of materials, labor, fuel, etc.; he computes that on the existing
price of goods he can make a certain profit ; possibly
he borrows money to carry on his business; when the
goods are ready for sale the price has gone down. The
farmer, the packer, every man who has to invest in the
present and look to the future for returns is similarly
affected by a falling market. Even bankers are frequently caught by the depreciation of the securities
they have taken. For example, we are told by monometallists that the recent great bank failures of Australia were due to speculation, booming, reckless backing
of enterprises, and the like, but Australian bankers

earnestly deny this. One of them, Mr. David Murray, says in a recent article :

The question is now forced upon us: Why is it that banking, which was carried on successfully and profitably from the earliest period of colonial history, has in these last days suffered such reverses? I think there is only one answer to the question, which is, the unaccountable and continuous fall in the value of all securities. "Clear-sighted and practical financiers" did not foresee it, and cannot account for it. Banks advanced on these securities at a safe margin, quite as safely as their advances were made twenty to thirty years ago. These margins have now disappeared. The produce of the colonies has fallen in value one-half. The estates, the runs, the mines, the farms, all producing factors, have fallen in a like ratio, not from scant production but from diminished prices.

There is another reason why banks have suffered largely in the last twenty years. A large portion of the profit of banking comes from loaning at interest the greater part of the money deposited by customers. In times of financial stringency and general panic bankers are forced to call in loans and hold heavy reserves as protection against possible runs. This means a loss of ordinary and legitimate profits to the bankers, as well as injury to customers, cramping of mercantile and manufacturing business, discharge of laborers, and general aggravation of the stringency. Did you ever consider how frequent and how severe these periods of stringency have been during the era of demonetized silver? Mr. Giffen noted it and conceded that it was due to the unusual demand for gold. Writing in the spring of 1885 he said :

The course of the money market since 1871, when the German government began to draw gold from London, has been full of such stringencies. The crisis of 1873 and 1875 were no doubt precipitated by them, and since 1876, in almost every year except 1879 and 1880, there has been a stringency of greater or less severity directly traceable to, or aggravated by the extraordinary demands for gold and the difficulty of supplying them.*

Eight years have passed since Mr. Giffen wrote this, but there has been no change in the frequent recurrence of these stringencies. The results have become more serious. The collapse of the Argentine Republic's effort to adopt a gold basis, and the the crisis produced by the Baring and Marietta failures, forced the true cause on the attention of financiers, even among the most obstinate of English monometallists. In 1892 Alfred de Rothschild, while insisting that the gold standard was absolutely necessary for England, wrote to the Brussels international monetary conference :

Gentlemen, I need hardly remind you that the stock of silver in the world is estimated at some thousands of millions, and if this conference were to break up without arriving at any definite result there would be a depreciation in the value of that commodity which it would be frightful to contemplate, and out of which a monetary panic would ensue, the far-spreading effects of which it would be impossible to foretell.†

The conference did not agree. The panic came. What a remarkable fulfillment of prophecy! And yet, looking back over it all, we see plainly that the prophet either did not fully understand or did not fully express the true cause. It is impossible that mere depreciation of value in silver should produce such results as have been produced. There has been no trouble in silver-standard countries. Gold-standard Australia, gold-standard United States, gold-standard England, gold-standard Italy and gold-standard Europe in general

*Note.—Essays on Fnance, 2d Series, p. 26.

†Note.—Proceedings, p. 72.

have suffered, but not silver standard countries. Why? Because the apparent depreciation of silver means an apparent depreciation of all prices. It is the appreciation of gold. The gold-standard countries are doing business on a falling market. This is the legitimate and necessary result of the policy of the doctrinaires of 1867. This is gold monometallism so far as it has been adopted. What of its further progress? When is the world to be free from this evil if the process continues? The history of the past twenty years furnishes some light. As the nations one after another transferred their burden of credit from silver to gold, gold appreciated. The same cause will produce the same effect. No wonder M. de Rothschild so earnestly urged Europe to join the United States in its effort to make an artificial demand for silver. No wonder Great Britain instructed its delegates to the Brussels conference " before concluding that matters must be left as they are, to examine with the greatest care any plan which may be submitted for the purpose of extending the monetary use of silver.* No wonder that Giffen writes : " Still more we ought to deprecate any change in silver-using countries in the direction of substituting gold for any part of the silver in use.''† The English monometallists now realize the truth of what Ernest Seyd wrote in 1871 : " It is a great mistake to suppose that the adoption of the gold valuation by other states besides England will be beneficial. It will only lead to the destruction of the monetary equilibrium hitherto existing, and cause a fall in the value of silver from which England's trade and the Indian silver valuation

*Note.—Proceedings, p. 113.

†Note.—Essays in Finance, 1st Series, p. 347.

will suffer more than all other interests, grievous as the general decline of prosperity all over the world will be."

The position of the English monometallists has been that England and a few other civilized countries ought to retain the gold standard, but semi-civilized countries—among which they seem to include the United States—ought to maintain the silver standard. An almost official declaration of this is found in Mr. Goschen's threat to the Paris monetary conference of 1878:

The *laissez faire* policy in India had done more than anything else to keep up the value of silver. If, however, other States were to carry on a propaganda in favor of a gold standard, and of the demonetization of silver, the Indian government would be obliged to reconsider its position, and might be forced by events to take measures similar to those taken elsewhere. In that case, the scramble to get rid of silver might provoke one of the gravest crises ever undergone by commerce. One or two States might demonetize silver without serious results, but if all demonetized there would be no buyers, and silver would fall in alarming proportions. * * * The American proposal for a universal double standard seemed impossible of realization, a veritable Utopia; but the theory of a universal gold standard was equally Utopian, and, indeed, involved a false Utopia. It was better for the world at large that the two metals should continue in circulation than that one should be universally substituted for the other. * * * At present there was a vicious circle; States were afraid of employing silver on account of the depreciation, and the depreciation continued because States refused to employ it. * * * It was not the fact of this stock of £15,000,000 (Germany's discarded silver) being in existence which depreciated prices so heavily. If this same sum were in the United States Treasury in place of an equal amount of gold, the aggregate stock of silver would be unaltered, but this £15,000,000 would no longer weigh on the market, and silver might be restored to a normal position. It was in this direction, and renouncing theoretical discussions, that the States interested ought rather to direct their efforts.*

NOTE.—Proceedings, p. 51.

Strange to say, our statesmen adopted this policy dictated by England. We put the £15,000,000 into our treasury, and we have put more than £60,000,000 more on top of it. While we were doing it, Egypt, Turkey, Roumania, and Austria-Hungary have gone to the gold standard, and Argentine Republic and India have attempted it. The appreciation of gold has gone steadily on. Our silver purchases did not, and could not, stop it, because we too had the gold standard, and no part of our burden of ultimate credit rested on the silver we coined. Now our eyes are partially opened, and we have decided that we will no longer be the cats-paw of England. There is not the slightest probability that the United States will resume the purchase system, and scarcely greater probability that it will serve England's purpose by making silver standard money until the nations of the earth generally do the same thing.

Neither is there any probability that the present silver standard countries will carry out the English idea by remaining on a silver basis. How can they be persuaded to do so? They need international money as well as the rest of the world. Already India has attempted to make the change. Mexico is growing restive, and feels that the premium of seventy-four per cent. on gold which it encounters in international transactions is an injury to its commerce. Japan and China are coming more and more under Occidental influences, and are ambitious to range themselves in the front ranks of civilization. They have adopted the most modern appliances in their navies and armies. They are educating their young men and young women in Europe and America. Thirty-five years ago Japan consented to open the doors to civilization. To-day the shops of Japan are furnished with telephones and lighted by electricity. Nay, more, as I write this chapter, the telegraphic dispatches announce that the Japanese government is considering ways and means for the adoption of the gold standard. It was a wild vagary—a disregard of all human experience—to imagine that these countries would stand against the greatest of all civilizing forces, the international medium of commerce. Their business interests protest daily against such a course, in the natural and irrepressible demand for a currency of universal and equal purchasing power. How can these countries be kept from the gold stanard? Will it be said that they are not strong enough to reach and hold it? They are stronger than the countries of Western Europe, because they are greater producers, and because their industries are not subjected to so crushing a weight of taxation. These causes never fail of their effects. France is the greatest natural producer of Western Europe, and France is now recognized as the strongest, financially, of nations. The agricultural nations can stand the strain of gold monometallism better than others. They have food. The nations that must break down first in this struggle are the manufacturing nations of Europe. There are but two possible terminations to the movement started by the monetary conference of 1867. One is the adoption of the gold standard by the entire world. The other is the adoption of international bimetallism.

Suppose the former results. Suppose we have reached the goal. Suppose that through gigantic losses and universal bankruptcy the world reaches a point where gold has attained its maximum limit of appreciation from this cause, and prices have touched their lowest point; have we gained or lost by the change? What are the advantages of the single gold standard when the world has it? The greatest excellence of any kind of money is stability, because money is a measure, and measures are of little use unless they are stable. Anyone can see the injury to business that would result from a yard-stick or a bushel that fluctuated constantly and violently in size, and that injury would be no greater than has been the injury from the fluctuation in the measure of value that has occurred in the past twenty years. If an universal single gold standard can be reached, would it be as stable as the bimetallic standard? For two reasons it is impossible that it should be. The first is that the contraction of the base on which credit rests necessarily makes it subject to more frequent and more violent fluctuations. If we should put this proposition in the reverse form and ask the question : "Does inflation of credit-money tend to stability?" no sane man would answer that it did. The contraction of the base on which credit rests is the same in effect as the extension of credit on an unchanged base. For illustration, if a country has a metallic fund of one hundred millions, and a paper issue of three hundred millions, everyone would doubt the safety of increasing the paper to six hundred millions, but the relation between the two would be the same in that case as if the paper were left unchanged and the metallic fund were reduced to fifty millions. The demonetization of silver is the exact equivalent of inflation, so far as stability is concerned, not only for the reason stated, but also because under it silver becomes credit-money which must be redeemed in gold. Monometallism and inflation are equivalents, and the increase of burden on the basis or standard will always cause greater fluctuation in the demand for, and value of, the standard as the expansion and contraction of credit occur.

In the second place the fluctuation of value in any commodity may in fact be greater or less than the fluctuation of average values, but the great desideratum in money is something that will remain as nearly as possible with the average of prices, because money is the medium of exchange, and exchange or barter is conducted with reference to average prices. In other words it is desirable that the money substance should be affected as little as possible by influences peculiar to itself, and not affecting other commodities. If it were possible to establish such a standard the average value of all commodities would be the fairest and best measure or standard of value. This is impossible, but it is possible to keep in a money system the principle of average value, or in other words to counteract to a large extent the natural fluctuation that belongs to any individual commodity. Necessarily the average value of two commodities is less affected by these individual causes than the values of the two commodities separately. If the two articles can be fastened together at a fixed ratio of exchange, as gold and silver may by universal bimetallism, the result will be a money whose value will be the average of the two. And even if, as monometallists contend, and as in fact occurred under the old bimetallism with different coinage ratios in different countries, a double standard results in the use of the cheaper metal to the exclusion of the dearer, the use of cheaper metal makes it dearer and the disuse of the dearer metal makes it cheaper, so that the two are naturally drawn together. Under either theory an average value of money is preserved that is more stable than the value of either metal alone, or of the two maintained separately as standards in different countries, as the English monometallists recommend.

This fact was understood and explained by economists before the period of demonetization, and the consequent new aspect of the discussion of bimetallism. In the "Investigations in Currency and Finance" written in 1862, but published after his death, Mr. Jevons found it necessary to defend his proof of a depreciation of the value of gold from 1850 to 1860 from the claim that if there had been such a depreciation it would be shown by comparison with silver. In reply he pointed to bimetallism in France, and said:

And so long as there is much silver coin current in France, and the law of the year 11 (establishing bimetallism) holds, it will be possible for merchants, by importing gold and exporting silver, to gain the difference of the natural and legal rates of value in France, *minus* charges of coinage, insurance, etc. Very correctly Chevalier argues that so long as this state of things lasts, it will be impossible at London, Brussels, Hamburg, or even at New York, or any other great center of commerce, for gold to fall in value much below that of fifteen and a half times its weight of silver. On these grounds he calls the French silver currency *a parachute which retards the fall of the value of gold.* Here is the great oversight. The French currency may and does prevent gold from falling much below its old *relative value to silver*, but it cannot prevent both gold and silver from falling in value. The inevitable conclusion drawn from my table of prices is that gold has fallen say nine per cent.; silver has risen in value compared with gold three per cent.; the difference, *six per cent., must necessarily represent the depreciation of silver.**

In fact, both Jevons and Chevalier are right.

NOTE.—P. 60.

Silver fell with gold, but retarded its fall. Not France alone, but the bimetallic world produced the result. As we have seen, silver and gold were prevented from coming immediately into harmony by the Oriental valuation of silver at a higher rate than the European valuation, and as this passed away the two came together again through the decade of the 60s., as may be seen from the table of ratios, Appendix 3. The ratio of 1870-1872, is practically the same as the ratio of 1850-1852, although the production of gold was still largely in excess of the production of silver at the later period, and the world's supply of gold, in relation to silver, had been almost doubled.

Another very strong argument against monometallism is its desertion by its adherents. A change of opinion on a mooted question by a single person amounts to little, but a strong trend in one direction among those who give special attention to a subject is very good evidence of the correctness of the position to which they come. At the international conference of 1867, there was but one delegate, Mr. Mees, the president of the Bank of the Netherlands, who protested against the single gold standard. The only other great banker who shared his views at that time, of whom I have knowledge, was Baron Alphonse de Rothschild, who said in 1869, " As a sequel, we should have to demonetize silver completely. That would be to destroy an enormous part of the world's capital; that would be ruin." The economists who took positions against the demonetization movement may be counted on the fingers. Prof. Wolowski, of the College de France. Cernuschi, and Ernest Seyd are the only ones of note. Even in 1872 and 1873, when the demonetization measure was before our Congress, not one member of that body raised his voice in defense of the principle of bimetallism, though this was perhaps due to oversight, as the large majority of the members certainly had no idea of the effect of the bill. What a change has occurred since then. In this country the most aggressive advocate of gold monometallism was Hon. John Sherman. He wrote to our delegate to the conference of 1867 strongly urging it, and condemning "the impossible effort of making two standards of value."* He, more than any other man, was responsible for this country's joining in the movement. And yet, on July 15, 1878, he wrote Mr. Groesbeck, one of our delegates to the conference of that year, as follows:

During the Monetary Conference in Paris, when silver in our country was excluded from circulation by being undervalued, I was strongly in favor of the single standard of gold, and wrote a letter, which you will find in the proceedings of that conference, stating briefly my view. At that time the wisest among us did not anticipate the sudden fall of silver or the rise of gold that has occurred. This uncertainty of the relation between the two metals is one of the chief arguments in favor of a monometallic system, but other arguments, showing the dangerous effect upon industry by dropping one of the precious metals from the standard of value, outweigh in my mind all theoretical objections to the bimetallic system. I am thoroughly convinced that if it were possible for the leading commercial nations to fix by agreement an arbitrary relation between silver and gold, even though the market value might vary somewhat from time to time, it would be a measure of the greatest good to all nations. My earnest desire is that you may succeed in doing this.†

To this sentiment I believe Mr. Sherman still adheres. At least he said in the Senate on May 31, 1892,

*Note.—Sen. Doc. 14, 2d Sess. 40th Cong., p. 107.
†Note.— Proceedings Paris Monetary Conf. of 1878, p. 136.

that "When the law of 1873 was passed the only trouble about it was that we were not as wise as the Almighty Ruler of the universe. We could not see ahead." And in a continuation of the same speech, on June 1, he said "I am willing to stand by the President, to aid him all we can in an international conference." We may claim, therefore, the conversion of the leader of the monometallist forces in America. Outranking Mr. Sherman as a financier, we have Hon. Hugh McCulloch, who, in 1867, was Secretary of the Treasury. He too supported the movement for gold monometallism, though not so actively as Mr. Sherman. He wrote to Mr. Ruggles, our delegate, congratulating "the conference on the result of its labors,"* and in his report of November 30, 1867, he referred the matter to Congress as "fully discussed in the separate report of Mr. Ruggles," specially indicating as one of the points made by Mr. Ruggles, "The necessity of a single standard exclusively of gold. The fallacy and impossibility of a double standard of gold and silver."† And yet, in 1887, Mr. McCulloch wrote this:

If Professor Sumner had been a banker at any time prior to 1848, he would not have gone so wide of the mark as he did in saying, in the 1885 June number of the North American Review, "We do not want or need silver as a circulating medium, and shall not abandon it, because we never had it." We did have it, and sooner or later we shall have it again, and without its being degraded. We are not prepared—the world is not prepared for the demonetization of either gold or silver, nor can this preparation be brought about without the wiping out of a very large part of public and private debts. Debts contracted when both metals are used as money would be a burden too heavy to be borne when measured by a single standard.‡

---

*NOTE.—Sen. Doc. 14, 2d Sess. 40th Cong , p. 82.
†NOTE.—Report, pp XLII and XLIII.
‡NOTE.—Men and Measures of Half a Century, p. 110.

When we pass to the lesser lights we find a veritable hegira from bimetallism. The congressmen of 1873, one after another, have declared that they did not understand or did not know the contents of the act of that year, and have disavowed faith in its provisions. And this not only of members whose attention was not specially called to it, but even members of the committees of the House and Senate who reported on it, and Mr. Kelley, who originally introduced the bill in the House, and who said in support of it : "All experience has shown that you must have one standard coin, which shall be a legal tender for all others, and then you may promote your domestic convenience by having a subsidiary coinage of silver." I do not believe that any one can point to a dozen Americans prominent in public life, who avow themselves believers in the principle of monometallism, though there are still a number of economists and financial writers who adhere to it.

The growth of bimetallist sentiment in other countries is quite as striking, when all conditions are considered. The international monetary conferences of 1878, 1881 and 1892 furnish conclusive proof of the world-wide belief that something ought to be done to change the existing condition, and the existing condition is gold monometallism, so far as international commerce is concerned. The preponderance of sentiment in all of these was for universal bimetallism, and it was a· growing preponderance. The educational effect of these conferences has been immense, and the world is under a debt of gratitude to Horton, Allard, Boïssevain and their colleagues, who have done so much to clear away the debris of ancient monetary fallacies and lay broad and deep the foundations of a real science. It is

natural that there should have been less progress in
Germany and England than elsewhere, for the people
of both countries are characterized by a pugnacious
obstinacy that is not easily reconciled to change, even
in the right direction. Neither can we overlook the
influence of two phenomenal men, Bismarck and Gladstone, strong in the glory of past achievements and in
present political power, who have resisted the movement. Bismarck, indeed, early expressed some disgust
at "the scramble for gold," and recently is said to have
been convinced of the error of gold monometallism.
Gladstone has sanctioned England's effort to induce
other countries to endeavor to rehabilitate silver, but
nothing more, and it is hardly to be expected that men
of strong character would change their views on such a
question in old age. Nevertheless bimetallism has been
winning its way in both countries. It is commonly
conceded that Germany will follow if England will
join in the movement for universal bimetallism.

One of the most striking conversions in England
was that of Henry Hucks Gibbs, director and former
governor of the Bank of England, delegate of England
to the conference of 1878. At that conference he avowed
himself "a partisan of the single gold standard," but
he subsequently had a complete change of view, and
became president of the English Bimetallic League. In
a public speech he said:

Mr. Goschen and I were together on the conference
in Paris; both of us were sturdy defenders of gold
monometallism, but I have changed my mind. I do
not say Mr. Goschen has changed his mind, but he has
somewhat modified it.

While Mr. Goschen does not avow conversion to
the principle of universal bimetallism he does announce

views that concede nearly everything that bimetallists claim. He has gone this far at a public meeting:

There is a class of monometallists who say that bimetallism is all nonsense, and they cannot understand what it means. Now, I do not think that it is nonsense at all. I think it is a very serious demand for a change, which, if adopted, would produce very large results. * * * The action of the Latin Union, the action of Germany, the displacement of silver and the enthronement of gold in its place, in many countries, have had an immense effect in producing the changes which bimetallists deplore and attempt to remedy. So far, it appears to me, it can fairly be said that the actions of governments have a distinct influence on the question of standards. I fully appreciate the importance of the question. I feel it almost impossible to exaggerate its importance.*

The view of Mr. Goschen here expressed appears to be very much the most common view of English politicians who advocate the gold standard. At any rate the Royal Commission on Gold and Silver, which reported in 1888, and which was composed of six monometallist and six bimetallists, assented unanimously to the following proposition:

Sec. 107. We think that in any conditions fairly to be contemplated in the future, so far as we can forecast them from the experience of the past, a stable ratio might be maintained if the nations we have alluded to† were to accept and strictly adhere to bimetallism, at the suggested ratio. We think that if in all these countries gold and silver could be freely coined, and thus become exchangeable against commodities at the fixed ratio, the market value of silver as measured by gold would conform to that ratio and not vary to any material extent.

It may be mentioned in this connection that since the report of this commission Mr. Leonard H. Court-

---

'Note—Proceedings Brussels Conference of 1892, p. 224.

†Note—The United Kingdom, Germany, the United States and the Latin Union.

ney, one of the monometallist members, has openly avowed his conversion to bimetallism.

Why, then, does not England consent to universal bimetallism? Simply because these politicians believe that the present condition is better for England because it is a creditor nation. Mr. Gladstone put it on that ground in the discussion of the question in Parliament in February 1893, and no one could have put it more bluntly. He said:

The honorable member spoke rather with ridicule upon the proposition of this country as the great creditor country of the world. It is the great creditor country of the world; of that there can be no doubt whatever; and it is increasingly the great creditor country of the world. ·I suppose there is not a year which passes over our heads which does not largely add to the mass of British investments abroad. I am almost afraid to estimate the total amount of the property which the United Kingdom holds beyond the limits of the United Kingdom; but of this I am well convinced, that it is not to be counted by tens or hundreds of millions.

One thousand millions probably would be an extremely low and inadequate estimate. Two thousand millions, or something even more than that, is very likely to be nearer the mark. ["Hear!" "Hear!"] I think under these circumstances it is a rather serious matter to ask this country to consider whether we are going to perform this supreme act of self-sacrifice. I have a profound admiration for cosmopolitan principles. I can go a great length in moderation [laughter] in recommending their recognition and establishment, but if there are these two thousand millions or fifteen hundred millions of money which we have got abroad, it is a very serious matter as between this country and other countries.

We have nothing to pay to them; we are not debtors at all; we should get no comfort, no consolation out of the substitution of an inferior material, of a cheaper money, which we could obtain for less and part with for more. We should get no consolation, but the consolation throughout the world would be great. [Loud laughter.]

This splendid spirit of philanthropy, which we can
not too highly prize, because I have no doubt all this is
foreseen, would result in our making a present of fifty
or a hundred millions to the world. It would be thank-
fully accepted, but I think the gratitude for your benev-
olence would be mixed with very grave misgivings
as to your wisdom.

Mr. Gladstone and his followers have the idea that
a money system which increases the burden of debt
benefits the creditor, and they will probably cling to it
unless the actual losses of the creditors, from the break-
ing down of debtors, show them their mistake. The year
1893 must have been very instructive to them. Of
course the English economists, who attempt to defend
monometallism on principle, cannot take such a position. Giffen was moved to such wrath by the conces-
sion of the Royal Commission quoted above, or, as he
says, by public men holding similar views, that he de-
clares " it is surely a scandal of the first magnitude that
men of light and leading in other respects should have
talked seriously, even if only for a moment, of any
such idea as the possibility of a fixed price between
gold and silver."* And this is about the only argument
left to Giffen's school unless we may so account his
further proposition : "The only way, then, to deal
with bimetallists is to refer them back to Adam Smith
and other expounders of the A B C of monetary
science."† And they do refer to Smith and Locke and
other authorities, seemingly oblivious to the fact that
these giants of their day were discussing the money
system of a single country when other countries were
maintaining diverse coinage ratios. They did not discuss
universal bimetallism at all. Their views are accepted

*Note.—Case Against Bimetallism, p. 131.
†Note.—*Ibid*, p. 207.

freely by the bimetallists of to-day as to mere national action, but we have come to a time when money must be recognized as an international, and not merely a national matter.

It must not be imagined, however, that all English economists follow Giffen. On the contrary the trend is strongly in the opposite direction. In proof of this I submit the following statement of Prof. H. S. Foxwell, the distinguished professor of political economy in University College, London, in his recently published letter to M. de Laveleye, the well known bimetallist:

Cambridge University: Professor Alfred Marshall, bimetallist; Professor Sidgwick, bimetallist. Edinburgh: Professor Nicholson, author of an excellent book on the subject, vice-president of the Bimetallic League. Oxford: Thorold Rogers admits the scarcity of gold, rejects bimetallism. University College of London: H. S. Foxwell, vice-president of the Bimetallic League. Nottingham: Professor J. E. Symes, bimetallist. Liverpool: Professor E. G. Gonner, vice-president of the Bimetallic League. Manchester: Professor J. E. Munro admits the bimetallic theory. London, King's College: Professor Edgeworth inclines towards bimetallism. * * * Whoever refuses to admit that a fixed ratio between gold and silver can be established and maintained by international treaty is no longer considered among us an economist.

This progress of bimetallism—this steady process of conversion of men who study the subject—in such marked contrast with the almost universal prevalence of the monometallist sentiment of 1867—is surely good evidence of the merit of the bimetallic theory, and it also gives ground for hope that the nations may soon be brought to the point of abandoning the folly of the past twenty years.

V.

THE REMEDIES PROPOSED.

It is not possible that events of the striking character heretofore noted as having occurred .in the past twenty years, and especially events so disastrous in their nature, should occur without attracting the general attention of statesmen, financiers and students of social economy. In all civilized nations they have been repeatedly considered in legislative bodies. Newspapers have found in them topics for extended discussion. The permanent literature on the subject has grown to great proportions. More significant than all these is the fact that since the monetary conference of 1867 three international monetary conferences have been held for the purpose of devising some cure for the existing evil, for the monetary conditions of the past twenty years are conceded on all sides to have been evil and productive of evil. Even more striking is the fact that monometallists as well as bimetallists maintain that there must be a more extended use of silver as money, or affairs will continue to grow worse. Naturally from this great amount of consideration there have come numerous propositions for relief, and though these vary greatly in their general character, as well as in detail, they all group logically in three classes, which we will now consider briefly.

The first class includes the various proposals for an extension of the use of silver, or its equivalent, as token money, on a gold basis. There are two facts common to all these plans that deserve special notice. The first is that these are the plans of the monometallists—monometallists, for though many who have favored such plans call themselves bimetallists, it is simply a contradiction of terms to speak of bimetallism on a monometallic basis. Any system that does not make silver a standard money—a money not ultimately redeemable in gold—is a monometallic system. The second is that only remedial plans of this character have been given any trial in the past twenty years, and they have all failed most dismally. Nor is this strange if we will but bear in mind the rudimentary principle which we have established that the cause of all the trouble was taking the burden of ultimate credit off from silver and placing it all upon gold. Necessarily no additional use of silver on which no burden of ultimate credit rests can relieve the pressure upon gold. On the contrary the more silver token-money there is issued the greater is the burden of credit that rests upon gold, and the greater the demand for and appreciation of gold. As we have already noted, the amount of silver coined in these twenty years has exceeded the amount produced, but gold has continued to appreciate notwithstanding this, and notwithstanding that more gold has been coined than has been produced.

The principal trial of plans of this class has been the purchase of silver by the United States under the Allison (or Bland) law of 1878, and the Sherman law of 1890. This policy, proposed as we have seen by Mr. Goschen, at the conference of 1878, was followed by this country for fifteen years. Under it we have accumulated in our treasury more than five times as much silver as he then thought would be necessary to restore the old equilibrium, but the market ratio has constantly gone farther and farther away from it. The reason is

simple. Both our laws provided for the purchase of
silver at the market rate, and coinage into token money
redeemable in gold. The market rate of silver, as we
have seen, has merely marked the general average of
gold prices, or in other words the appreciation of gold,
and the purchase of silver has no effect of retarding
this; but the coinage of silver as token money, or the
issue of notes against silver bullion, adds to the burden
of credit resting on gold, and appreciates it still more.
Hence the policy which we have so persistently followed
has aggravated the evil instead of remedying it, and if
the nations had adopted the advice of Rothschild at the
conference of 1892, the situation would have been so
much the worse.

Second in importance only to this, is the plan of
issuing no bank notes or other paper currency of small
denominations, and thereby forcing a more extended
use of silver in the small transactions which make up
the great bulk of the world's business. This plan has
been followed by the States of the Latin Union and
some other European powers, and is advocated by many
monometallist "friends of silver" in this country. This
plan is not harmful, for the reason that the burden of
credit placed on gold by the issue of such silver token
money is certainly no greater than the burden of the
paper money it displaces; but at the same time it is
utterly without effect, for the reasons mentioned above,
in retarding the appreciation of gold or the depreciation of silver. The silver so issued is not standard
money—not money of ultimate payment—and is floated
only by being constantly redeemable in gold by the
government that issues it.

Another proposition of this class which has been

received with considerable favor in this country, is Secretary Windom's scheme for issuing government notes against deposits of silver bullion, redeemable in silver bullion at its market value when the notes are presented. A moment's thought will show any one that this plan is based on the hypothesis that the source of the money trouble is a decline of silver—not an appreciation of gold. If this hypothesis were correct, this plan would probably tend to remedy the evil, but it is not correct. What effect could such a plan have in reducing the purchasing power of gold? Obviously none. The whole transaction is on a gold basis. Silver is deposited at its gold value, and paper is issued on it at the same rate. The paper is redeemable in silver bullion at its gold value. If gold continues to appreciate, as it certainly will under existing influences, the government would have to purchase enough silver bullion to cover the depreciation, or, what is equivalent, redeem in gold. This could have no more effect on the movement of gold than would the deposit of wheat, or diamonds, or any other commodity, under similar circumstances. It is mere warehouse business, with the disadvantages of subjecting the country to unlimited inflation and possibly sudden contraction of the volume of currency. The fundamental fallacy of all plans of this class is that they are not aimed at the real evil, but at an imaginary one.

The plans of the second class include all propositions for free coinage of silver, at a fixed ratio, by individual nations, and this proposal has received very earnest support in the United States. At the present time most of the intelligent advocates of this plan concede that the inevitable result of its trial would be silver monometallism, but insist that silver monometallism is preferable to gold monometallism. If this were the only choice, and there were in fact no hope of a general restoration of bimetallism, we might reasonably agree with them, for certainly a standard that under existing circumstances must move with the movement of average prices is much more desirable than a standard under which prices are utterly unsettled, and under which no man can do business with any certainty of results. It is hardly worth while to enter into any argument to show that the necessary result of the free coinage of silver by this country alone would be silver monometallism. Our own experience has shown us that we could not maintain actual bimetallism when our coinage ratio varied but a fraction from a comparatively uniform market ratio. Our gold was carried away under our early overvaluation of silver, and our silver was carried away under our later overvaluation of gold. If any further proof were needed of the utter impossibility of maintaining bimetallism under the present extreme and violently fluctuating market ratio it may be found in the examples of the States of the Latin Union, which were obliged to abandon the attempt, or our neighbor, Mexico, under whose bimetallic laws silver monometallism is an accomplished result. The only question that is open, in connection with a proposal for free coinage by a single nation, is whether silver monometallism is desirable.

The greatest objection to it is that it would not be a settlement of the money trouble. It would leave us farther from the money of international commerce than we have ever been, and it would leave us subject to the constantly recurring demand for money that is good everywhere. This demand comes chiefly from the mercantile classes, but unquestionably there is an earnest desire among all classes, in the United States for money that is good in any part of the world—money that does not rest on credit—just as there is in all civilized countries. Indeed one great cause of objection to our present system of gold monometallism, with silver token money, is that we do not have "an honest dollar"—a dollar that is good all round the world. Our eagle, double eagle, half-eagle, and quarter-eagle, are good everywhere, but our dollar is worth only about sixty cents as soon as it goes beyond our boundaries, except where affected by a prospective return to them. This objection is not made by gold monometallists alone, but by bimetallists also. As Mr. Beith put it, on behalf of the bimetallists of England, at the meeting at Manchester, on October 27, 1892 : "We ask that the government shall take measures in concert with the other great nations of the world, to arrange one money for the commerce of the world—that is, that the Queen's shilling, the Queen's rupee, and the Queen's dollar, shall run as freely as the Queen's sovereign, in every part of the Queen's empire, and of the world." This is a demand that is urged both by the needs of commerce and by national pride, and there is no reason for supposing that either will be less potent in the future than at present.

If now we should pass to silver monometallism this objection would be still more forcible. Under the present system we maintain relations with the money of international commerce by constantly redeeming our silver money in gold, or in other words, maintaining it on a parity with gold; but under silver monometallism we

would entirely abandon the money of international
commerce, and our own money would become merely a
commodity to the commercial world, as Mexico's money
now is. There would of course result at least a temporary increase in the value of silver, or rather a
decrease in the purchasing power of gold, if we were to
transfer our burden of credit from gold to silver, but it
could not be very large, and it would probably be
quickly overcome by other nations passing from the
silver to the gold standard. Our dollar would be worth
as much abroad as at home, but it would be worth only
the bullion value of the silver in it anywhere, and the
discrepancy between this and the value of the gold
coins in multiples of its denomination would be a continual cause of dissatisfaction. Gold would be "at a
premium," and the continual clamor which this would
produce would prevent an adherence to the system.
This is not a speculative assertion. During the past
twenty years we have seen this influence turn nation
after nation from the silver standard to the gold
standard, and even now the desire for money of the
commercial world's standard is so strong in the remaining silver standard countries that they will certainly
attempt the gold standard unless international bimetallism is speedily accomplished. In the United States the
demand for money of this quality is now so decided that
a silver standard could scarcely be considered a possibility even if it were in other respects desirable.

Beyond this lies the further consideration that this
remedy is not sufficient for the disorder. Unless all the
conclusions that we have reached in these pages are
erroneous, and unless all the bimetallists and advocates
of silver are mistaken, the existing disorder is a result

of the appreciation of gold, not a depreciation of silver. No remedy can be effective unless it brings gold back to its former relation to average prices. That relation was destroyed not by the demonetization of silver by any one country, but by a general demonetization by the leading commercial nations. It can be restored only by a system which will again place the burden of credit equally on gold and silver throughout the world. Of course no one country could accomplish this by going to a silver standard, but it is urged that if a strong nation like the United States were to lead the way to bimetallism other countries would follow. It is not to be supposed that they would follow until they saw the result of our attempt, and if the United States were to attempt free coinage of silver, and go to a silver standard as it necessarily must, the result would discourage other nations from attempting a similar course. They would see our attempted bimetallism a failure. They would see us shut out from the money of the commercial world. Instead of leading the way we should block the way. Hence, as a step towards the restoration of bimetallism, towards the rehabilitation of silver, towards the readjustment of prices, free coinage by any one country, under existing circumstances, would be an error. Our opportunity to lead is in the way of inducing other nations to take the step with us.

The third class of propositions includes those which call for bimetallism, either universal or by a number of countries in league under conditions that will tend to produce universal bimetallism. The objection at once made to these is that other countries will not join—that England and Germany at least would stand out against a proposition of this character. This objection has been

considered sufficient in the past. Probably it is sufficient still to prevent an immediate universal arrange-
ment. It is primarily a question whether the experience of 1893 has been enough to convince the moneyed
power of England that the creditor is benefited by the
prosperity of the debtor. But, supposing that a present
universal agreement is impossible, may not that end be
ultimately reached by a present league or union of the
nations that desire a restoration of bimetallism? This
would depend on two questions : (1.) Could a league
be formed that would be strong enough? (2.) Could
the league nations protect themselves against the drain
of gold to the non-league countries that would naturally result under the economic laws which have been
heretofore explained? It seems probable from the sentiment expressed in the later international monetary conferences, and from existing national relations, that the
countries of the Latin Union, Russia, Spain, Holland,
China, Japan, Mexico, and all of Central and South
America would join in such a league if an affirmative
answer could be given to the second question. And
these nations are certainly strong enough, with the
United States, to maintain bimetallism if that drain of
gold can be prevented. How can it be prevented? As
we have seen it always arises from a difference in money
systems that permits of a profit from commerce in
money—from making one of the money metals a commodity. If such a league were formed, the drain of
gold from league to non-league countries would naturally occur in the form of a practically direct exchange
of silver for gold. This could easily be prevented by
imposing on all silver, coined or uncoined, imported
from non-league countries, a duty higher than the differ-

ence between the market value of silver and its coinage value in the league countries. This would not only prevent an exchange of silver for gold, but would also necessitate the payment in gold or commodities for all goods shipped from league countries to non-league countries, and therefore create a flow of gold to the league countries.

If this plan were adopted there would still remain three causes for export of gold from league countries to non-league countries : (1.) The payment of existing debts in gold. (2.) The shipment of gold for loan purposes under influence of a high interest rate in non-league countries, or for other ordinary money purposes. (3.) The payment of gold for goods. The first of these could not well be prevented, so far as gold contracts are concerned, but it is not an item of sufficient importance to cause apprehension. The second would be self-compensating, because all such movements would be in the nature of loans, and would have to be repaid in kind. The third is the most important, and it might be prevented either by imposing prohibitory duties on the imports from non-league countries, or duties sufficiently high to discourage trade with them, and turn the trade of the league countries to each other. In other words, shut England and Germany, and their dependencies out from the commerce of the remainder of the world.

It will be objected that such a system would be one of coercion. This is true, but it would be a coercion arising entirely from self-defense against nations which insist on making an illegitimate profit out of money— illegitimate because money as the medium of commerce is properly a measure. There should be no more possibility of making a commercial profit from money

than there should be from an open and avowed altera-
tion of any other measure. A dishonest dollar is as
dishonest as a dishonest yardstick. A fluctuating dollar is as great an evil as a fluctuating yardstick. The
whole world is interested in having money as stable as
possible, and when England objects to what her Royal
Commission has agreed would give stability, solely on
the ground that as a creditor nation an abnormally
appreciated money is a national advantage to her, England loses all moral right to object to coercive measures. As a matter of course such a division of the
world would not last long. England and Germany
cannot exist without the commerce of the world—at
least not so easily as the world can exist without them.
To save themselves they would be obliged to join in the
movement, and so universal bimetallism would be ultimately secured.

And universal bimetallism is worth a determined
effort. As the world now stands it has two standards of
value, gold and silver, and when any nation passes from
one to the other the whole world feels the shock. No
nation can control its own measure of value while this
condition lasts. Did you ever consider the enormous
significance of this fact? The United States adopted
the gold standard in 1873, and the effect of that movement certainly did not last longer than 1879, when we
actually came to the gold standard by the resumption
of specie payments. And yet since then we have been
subjected to renewed appreciation of our standard and
renewed falls of prices as other countries came to the
same standard, although we have made most strenuous
efforts to prevent the appreciation of one metal by buying another. It may be objected, however, that our

efforts to befriend silver have caused our troubles. Very well. Look at England. It has been steadily true to the golden idol. It has not been trying to bolster up silver. It has not altered its standard by any act of its own. And yet the action of other countries has altered its standard and made a fall of prices similar to that in this country. There is no way at present to prevent any country from adopting any standard it likes, and if one desires a change the rest of the world has no choice but to endure the consequences. There is but one way to be free from this evil, and that is for the nations to come to a common standard, and adhere to it. There is no possibility that such standard should be either metal alone. It must be both, or we must remain as we are.

If universal bimetallism could be attained through the preliminary step of a bimetallic league, as proposed, it would be more beneficial than a direct advance to that condition, for two reasons. In the first place, a league once formed, with features of protection and coercion, would serve to perpetuate bimetallism after it was secured. It would afford the means of speedy punishment, by commercial exclusion, to any nation that abandoned the league agreement. This is of importance, because one of the objections commonly urged to international bimetallism is the declaration that there could be no means of enforcing the agreement if any nation should violate it. If commercial exclusion could force England and Germany into agreement, it would certainly be sufficient to prevent any nation from abandoning the agreement. In the second place, a league compact would require fixed rules and a representative body to enforce them, and to pass on questions of concern to the league. This would inevitably lead to further steps towards international unity and that "brotherhood of man" which is to the best minds the ideal development of the human race. Indeed, international money, of itself, would have an effect in that direction that could hardly be overrated. The race differences that separate mankind are chiefly mere matters of custom, and this is one matter of universal importance, and which is daily and hourly forced on the notice of all people, in which varying customs could easily and profitably be made uniform. Success in it would be strong inducement to attempt similar reform in other matters. It is, therefore, The World's Silver Question in the broadest sense of the term.

APPENDIX I.

THE WORLD'S PRODUCTION AND COINAGE OF GOLD AND SILVER FROM 1873 TO 1892.

(Special Report of Bureau of the Mint, August 28, 1893.)

Calendar Year.	GOLD.		SILVER.	
	PRODUCTION.	COINAGE.	PRODUCTION.	COINAGE.
1873	$112,563,249	$257,630,802	$94,126,214	$131,544,464
1874	104,674,672	135,778,387	95,676,214	102,931,232
1875	102,935,769	205,340,209	90,076,214	123,143,842
1876	110,318,358	213,119,278	96,600,775	123,577,164
1877	113,947,173	173,675,555	81,040,665	78,402,648
1878	119,092,786	188,386,611	94,882,177	161,191,913
1879	107,385,421	90,752,811	89,080,680	104,888,313
1880	106,436,786	149,725,081	96,704,978	84,611,974
1881	103,023,078	147,015,275	102,168,354	108,010,086
1882	101,996,640	99,697,170	111,802,337	110,785,934
1883	95,392,000	104,845,114	115,088,000	109,306,705
1884	101,694,000	99,432,795	110,773,000	95,832,084
1885	108,435,600	95,757.582	118,445,150	126,764,574
1886	106,163,877	94,642,070	120,626,800	124,854,101
1887	105,774,955	124,992,465	124,280,978	163,411,397
1888	110,196,915	134,828,853	140,706,413	134,922,344
1889	123,489,200	168,901,519	162,159,200	139,242,595
1890	120,465,300	149,095,865	173,743,000	151,032,820
1891	126,158,800	119,310,014	186,174,200	135,508,083
Totals ...	$2,080,144,579	$2,752,927,456	$2,204,155,349	$2,309,962.273

MONETARY SYSTEMS AND APPROXIMATE STOCKS OF MONEY IN THE AGGREGATE IN THE PRINCIPAL COUNTRIES OF THE WORLD.

(The figures are those of the Mint Report of August 16, 1893.)

Countries.	Actual Standard	Ratio be-tween gold and full le-gal tender silver.	Ratio be-tween gold and limited tender sil-ver.	Popula-tion.	Stock of gold.	Stock of Silver.			Uncovered paper.
						Full tender.	Limited tender.	Total.	
United States	Gold	1 to 15.98	1 to 14.95	67,000,000	$604,000,000	$538,000,000	$77,000,000	$615,000,000	$412,000,000
United Kingdom	Gold	1 to 15½	1 to 14.28	38,000,000	550,000,000	100,000,000	100,000,000	100,000,000	50,000,000
France	Gold		1 to 14.38	39,000,000	800,000,000	650,000,000	50,000,000	700,000,000	81,402,000
Germany	Gold		1 to 13.957	49,500,000	640,000,000	103,000,000	108,000,000	211,000,000	107,000,000
Belgium	Gold	1 to 15½	1 to 14.38	6,100,000	65,000,000	48,400,000	6,600,000	55,000,000	54,000,000
Italy	Gold	1 to 15½	1 to 14.38	31,000,000	93,605,000	16,000,000	34,200,000	50,200,000	163,471,000
Switzerland	Gold	1 to 15½	1 to 14.38	3,000,000	15,000,000	11,400,000	3,600,000	15,000,000	14,000,000
Greece	Gold	1 to 15½	1 to 14.38	2,200,000	2,000,000	1,800,000	2,200,000	4,000,000	14,000,000
Spain	Gold	1 to 15½	1 to 14.38	18,000,000	40,000,000	120,000,000	38,000,000	158,000,000	100,000,000
Portugal	Gold		1 to 14.08	5,000,000	40,000,000		10,000,000	10,000,000	45,000,000
Austria-Hungary	Gold	1 to 15½	1 to 13.69	40,000,000	40,000,000	90,000,000		90,000,000	260,000,000
Netherlands	Gold		1 to 15	4,500,000	25,000,000	61,980,000	3,200,000	65,000,000	40,000,000
Scandinavian Union	Gold		1 to 14.88	8,600,000	32,000,000		10,000,000	10,000,000	27,000,000
Russia	Silver		1 to 15	113,000,000	250,000,000	22,000,000	38,000,000	60,000,000	500,000,000
Turkey	Gold	1 to 15.1	1 to 15.1	33,000,000	50,000,000		45,000,000	45,000,000	
Australia	Gold		1 to 14.28	4,000,000	100,000,000		7,000,000	7,000,000	
Egypt	Gold		1 to 15.68	7,000,000	100,000,000		15,000,000	15,000,000	
Mexico	Silver	1 to 16½		11,600,000	5,000,000	50,000,000		50,000,000	2,000,000
Central America	Silver	1 to 15½		3,000,000		500,000		500,000	2,000,000
South America	Silver	1 to 15½		25,000,000	45,000,000	25,000,000		25,000,000	600,000,000
Japan	Silver	1 to 16.18		40,000,000	90,000,000	50,000,000		50,000,000	56,000,000
India	Gold*	1 to 21		255,000,000		900,000,000		900,000,000	28,000,000
China	Silver			400,000,000		700,000,000		700,000,000	
The Straits						100,000,000		100,000,000	
Canada	Gold	1 to 14.95	1 to 15½	4,500,000	16,000,000		5,000,000	5,000,000	40,000,000
Cuba, Hayti, etc.	Gold		1 to 15½	2,000,000	20,000,000	1,200,000	800,000	2,000,000	40,000,000
Total					$3,582,605,000	$3,489,100,000	$553,600,000	$4,042,700,000	$2,635,873,000

*This depends, of course, on the maintenance of the order for the redemption of the rupee at 1s. 4d. gold.

APPENDIX 3.

THE MARKET RATIO OF GOLD TO SILVER FROM 1867 TO THE PRESENT.

(The figures to 1893 are from the Report of the Director of the Mint)

Year	Ratio	Year	Ratio	Year	Ratio	Year	Ratio	Year	Ratio
1687	14.94	1729	14.92	1771	14.66	1813	16.25	1855	15.38
1688	14.94	1730	14.81	1772	14.52	1814	15.04	1856	15.38
1689	15.02	1731	14.94	1773	14.62	1815	15.26	1857	15.27
1690	15.02	1732	15.09	1774	14.62	1816	15.28	1858	15.38
1691	14.98	1733	15.18	1775	14.72	1817	15.11	1859	15.19
1692	14.92	1734	15.39	1776	14.55	1818	15.35	1860	15.29
1693	14.83	1735	15.41	1777	14.54	1819	15.33	1861	15.50
1694	14.87	1736	15.18	1778	14.68	1820	15.62	1862	15.35
1695	15.02	1737	15.02	1779	14.80	1821	15.95	1863	15.37
1696	15.00	1738	14.91	1780	14.72	1822	15.80	1864	15.37
1697	15.20	1739	14.91	1781	14.78	1823	15.84	1865	15.44
1698	15.07	1740	14.94	1782	14.42	1824	15.82	1866	15.43
1699	14.94	1741	14.92	1783	14.48	1825	15.70	1867	15.57
1700	14.81	1742	14.85	1784	14.70	1826	15.76	1868	15.59
1701	15.07	1743	14.85	1785	14.92	1827	15.74	1869	15.60
1702	15.52	1744	14.87	1786	14.96	1828	15.78	1870	15.57
1703	15.17	1745	14.98	1787	14.92	1829	15.78	1871	15.57
1704	15.22	1746	15.13	1788	14.65	1830	15.82	1872	15.63
1705	15.11	1747	15.26	1789	14.75	1831	15.72	1873	15.92
1706	15.27	1748	15.11	1790	15.04	1832	15.73	1874	16.17
1707	15.44	1749	14.80	1791	15.05	1833	15.93	1875	16.59
1708	15.41	1750	14.55	1792	15.17	1834	15.73	1876	17.88
1709	15.31	1751	14.39	1793	15.00	1835	15.80	1877	17.22
1710	15.22	1752	14.54	1794	15.37	1836	15.72	1878	17.94
1711	15.29	1753	14.54	1795	15.55	1837	15.83	1879	18.40
1712	15.31	1754	14.48	1796	15.65	1838	15.85	1880	18.05
1713	15.24	1755	14.68	1797	15.41	1839	15.62	1881	18.16
1714	15.13	1756	14.94	1798	15.59	1840	15.62	1882	18.19
1715	15.11	1757	14.87	1799	15.74	1841	15.70	1883	18.64
1716	15.09	1758	14.85	1800	15.68	1842	15.87	1884	18.57
1717	15.13	1759	14.15	1801	15.46	1843	15.93	1885	19.41
1718	15.11	1760	14.14	1802	16.26	1844	15.85	1886	20.78
1719	15.09	1761	14.54	1803	15.41	1845	15.92	1887	21.13
1720	15.04	1762	15.27	1804	15.41	1846	15.90	1888	21.99
1721	15.05	1763	14.99	1805	15.79	1847	15.80	1889	22.09
1722	15.17	1764	14.70	1806	15.52	1848	15.85	1890	19.76
1723	15.20	1765	14.83	1807	15.43	1849	15.78	1891	20.92
1724	15.11	1766	14.80	1808	16.08	1850	15.70	1892	23.72
1725	15.11	1767	14.85	1809	15.96	1851	15.46	1893	
1726	15.15	1768	14.80	1810	15.77	1852	15.59	June	33.34
1727	15.24	1769	14.72	1811	15.53	1853	15.33	Aug	28.75
1728	15.11	1770	14.62	1812	16.11	1854	15.33	Oct	28.25

MASSACRES OF THE MOUNTAINS.

A History of the Indian Wars of the Far West.

By JACOB PIATT DUNN.

A FEW PRESS OPINIONS.

A volume which in completeness of detail and historical value, has no equal in American literature.—*Keynote, New York.*

Of the many volumes which have been written on our Indian wars, this of Mr. Dunn is entitled to rank among the best, if not as the very best.—*Critic, New York.*

A book which embodies a great deal of research, recounts much straightforward history, and furnishes enough of romance, tragedy, and pathos to stir by turns the reader's interest, pity, and indignation.—*Literary World, Boston.*

The most authentic and complete narrative we possess of the Indian wars.—*Globe, Boston.*

A credit to the author and a valuable contribution to the literature of our country.—*Standard, Chicago.*

Full of interest.—*Lutheran Observer, Philadelphia.*

Should go into the district school libraries.—*Press, Troy* (*N. Y.*)

A volume on a broad plan—so broad as to stand by itself in recent literature. We cannot suppress our high appreciation of the excellence of the volume.—*Post, Hartford.*

Of fascinating interest and much value.—*Literary Mirror, Williamstown.*

The chapters on the wars of Colorado will not be disputed by a single resident of the State.—*Times-Republican, Denver.*

An historical work of permanent interest and value.—*News, Indianapolis.*

A book of great value to the student of American history, and of permanent interest to the general reader.—*Chronicle, San Francisco.*

Published by HARPER & BROS.   Profusely illustrated;
pp. x., 784; 8vo, illuminated cloth; price $3.75.

INDIANA.

A REDEMPTION FROM SLAVERY.

By JACOB PIATT DUNN.

A FEW PRESS OPINIONS.

" Excepting Prof. Johnston's 'Connecticut' we may pronounce this the most scholarly of the series. It certainly ranks in the very first grade."—*The Critic, New York.*

" We can recommend Mr. Dunn's book as a careful and dispassionate study of a department of National history nowhere else so fully analyzed."—*Tribune, New York.*

It is essentially a historic monograph, and a model of works of its class. It is clear, strong, and convincing, showing mature study and patient research.—*Christian Intelligencer, New York.*

The volume is in every respect one of the most valuable of an exceedingly valuable series.—*Traveller, Boston.*

His style is good, he is apt in citation of authorities, he takes broad views, and he has a philosophical aim.—*Beacon, Boston.*

Mr. Dunn's methods are clear and logical.—*Record, Philadelphia.*

In writing a book on his own State, Mr. Dunn has evidently taken special pride in making it as attractive as possible. For years he has delved among the archives of the Indiana Historical Society, of which he is an officer, and into the literature bearing upon the early, romantic period in Indiana's history, until he has been able to give to many of his pages the fascination of a fairy tale.—*Capitol, Washington.*

The story is beautifully told. Home life is represented. Customs and dress and methods of labor are described. We have a genuine history of the first people of that great region.—*Public Opinion.*

At times his history is as absorbing as a novel.—*Crayon Bleu.*

The author writes with a firm grasp on his subject, and shows the growth and development of his State in a very brilliant and spirited manner.—*Chronicle, Quebec, Canada.*

Published by HOUGHTON, MIFFLIN & CO., in American Commonwealth series. Map, pp. viii., 453; 8vo, cloth; price $1.25.

www.ingramcontent.com/pod-product-compliance
Lightning Source LLC
Chambersburg PA
CBHW031446270326
41930CB00007B/882